Design for

Sustainable

Change

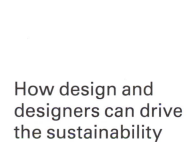

How design and
designers can drive
the sustainability
agenda

Required Reading Range
Course Reader

Anne Chick
Paul Micklethwaite

ava
academia

D0322314

Design for
sustainable
change

An AVA Book

Published by AVA Publishing SA
Rue des Fontenailles 16
Case Postale
1000 Lausanne 6
Switzerland
Tel: +41 786 005 109
Email: enquiries@avabooks.com

Distributed by Thames & Hudson (ex-North America)
181a High Holborn
London WC1V 7QX
United Kingdom
Tel: +44 20 7845 5000
Fax: +44 20 7845 5055
Email: sales@thameshudson.co.uk
www.thamesandhudson.com

Distributed in the USA & Canada by:
Ingram Publisher Services Inc.
1 Ingram Blvd.
La Vergne TN 37086
USA
Tel: +1 866 400 5351
Fax: +1 800 838 1149
Email: customer.service@ingrampublisherservices.com

English Language Support Office
AVA Publishing (UK) Ltd.
Tel: +44 1903 204 455
Email: enquiries@avabooks.com

© AVA Publishing SA 2011

ISBN 978-2-940411-30-6

Library of Congress Cataloging-in-Publication Data
Chick, Anne; Micklethwaite, Paul.
Design for Sustainable Change: How Design and Designers Can Drive the Sustainability Agenda / Anne Chick,
Paul Micklethwaite p. cm.
Includes bibliographical references and index.
ISBN: 9782940411306 (pbk.:alk.paper)
eISBN: 9782940439775
1.Sustainable design--Study and teaching.2.Sustainability--Study and teaching.3.Design--Social aspects.

NK1520 .C553 2011

10 9 8 7 6 5 4 3 2 1

Production by AVA Book Production Pte. Ltd., Singapore
Tel: +65 6334 8173
Fax: +65 6259 9830
Email: production@avabooks.com.sg

This book was printed on certified paper, which comes from responsible sources.

Printed in China

MIX
Paper from
responsible sources
FSC® C001701
www.fsc.org

Design for

Sustainable

Change

Required Reading Range
Course Reader

How design and
designers can drive
the sustainability
agenda

Anne Chick
Paul Micklethwaite

ethical:
aware-
ness/
reflect-
ion/
debate

ava
academia

Design for
sustainable
change

Contents

Contents

4

Part I
From design to
design thinking to
design activism

12

Chapter 1
Design is to
design a design to
produce a design

14

Chapter 2
Design thinking

34

Chapter 3
Design activism

56

Part II
Sustainability

74

Introduction

6

About the authors

8

How to get
the most out of
this book

10

1.1
Design as a field

16

1.2
Design as an
action or process

18

1.3
Design as a
concept or
proposal

20

1.4
Design as an
outcome

22

1.5
Design is an
attitude not a
profession

24

1.6
Design innovation
and the innovation
of design

32

2.1
Societal
challenges are
design challenges

36

2.2
From
problem-solving to
problem-setting

38

2.3
Service design:
maybe we don't
need a product?

42

2.4
Participatory
design: from
designing for to
designing with

46

2.5
Open source
design

50

2.6
There's nothing
new about design
thinking?

54

3.1
Design activism

58

3.2
Activism through
design

62

3.3
Design altruism

66

4

Part III
Design for
sustainable
change
100

5

6

7

Conclusion
166

Chapter 4
The 'S' word
76

Chapter 5
Sustainability
and design
102

Chapter 6
Design for
sustainable
living
118

Chapter 7
Design for
development
142

Bibliography
168

4.1
What do we want
to sustain?
78

5.1
Green design:
a single-issues
approach
104

6.1
Designing
sustainable
behaviour
120

7.1
Designing against
inequality
144

Further
resources
170

4.2
Models of
sustainability
80

5.2
Ecodesign: life-
cycle thinking
106

6.2
Designing
sustainable
systems
122

7.2
Designing for
needs, not wants
146

Index
174

4.3
Measuring
sustainability
84

5.3
Corporate social
responsibility
(CSR)
and design
112

6.3
Designing
sustainable
lifestyles
124

7.3
Approaches to
designing for
development
148

Picture credits
178

4.4
Sustainability is
not about single
issues
90

5.4
Design for
sustainability:
radical innovations
114

6.4
Designing
sustainable cities
134

Thanks
180

4.5
Types of capital
in sustainable
development
92

6.5
Designing
sustainable
regions
138

Working
with ethics
181

4.6
Should we use the
'S' word?
96

Introduction

This book explores how design thinking and design-led innovation can help us to address the sustainability agenda. It examines how design can provide methodologies for driving sustainable change in businesses, social organizations and wider society.

This is a book about how design is evolving and being applied to an increasing range of social and environmental challenges. Our ideas about what design is, are changing and design is adapting to participate in new arenas. Designers are also evolving, and developing greater 'design mindfulness' (in John Thackara's phrase[1]) in relation to what they do and how they do it.

An increasing number of books examine sustainable design, or design for sustainability. This book looks at design thinking as an approach – and an attitude – which by its nature considers issues of sustainability. This is not a book on 'sustainable design' or 'design for sustainability'.

**Part I
From design to
design thinking to
design activism**

**Part II
Sustainability**

**Part III
Design for
sustainable
change**

Part I looks at the recent emergence of 'design thinking' and 'design activism' as terms. Design has come to be recognized as an important and powerful tool as we strive for greater ecological and societal sustainability. Use of this tool should not be restricted to the design professions and the industries they serve. Design thinking looks beyond these confines to suggest a wider role for design in addressing bigger societal challenges. Through design thinking we can address transforming our societies and the ways we live, with particular reference to the sustainability agenda. Design activism goes even further in suggesting more radical ways to drive the changes we want to bring about.

Part II looks at the often hugely problematic concept of sustainability. The 'S' word can often mystify more than illuminate our thoughts on where we want our society to go. Confusion as to what sustainability is can hamper our attempts to respond to it as an agenda. This is true in relation to design as much as to any other activity, sector or discipline. This section aims to demystify the idea of sustainability.

Part III looks at how the two spheres of design and sustainability interrelate. If design is an important tool in our contemporary focus on sustainability, how is it being used? In what ways is design – through design craft, design thinking and design activism – driving sustainable change?

The sustainability agenda asks fundamental questions of design; this section explores recent real-life examples that demonstrate this.

[1] Thackara (2005:226)

When we use these terms as labels for a particular type or category of design, we run the risk of treating them as different from mainstream design. Sustainable design should be an essential element of 'good' design.

This book explores current best practice in the application of design thinking to tackling sustainability challenges. We argue that this wider application can allow us to realize the full potential of design as an agent of sustainable change. The sustainability agenda provides us with a fantastic opportunity to ask fundamental questions of design itself. What do we design? Why do we design? How do we design? We invite you to join us in thinking critically about what 'design' and 'sustainability' are, and how the two interrelate.

Our approach

This book presents debates around design and sustainability – and their interaction – as they are currently happening and as evident in recent real-life examples.

We aim to present not just the outcomes of these examples, but also how they were done, which is usually through interdisciplinary collaboration. The examples we present don't provide definitive conclusions to the continuing debates around design and sustainability. They represent the varied – and sometimes conflicting – ways in which the design agenda and the sustainability agenda interact and inform each other.

We aim to be constructively critical in presenting these recent examples of design for sustainable change. We have included differences of opinion and dissenting voices. We want to ask; what are our featured examples really about? What do they actually achieve? What might be their unanticipated outcomes?

We invite you the reader to identify your own queries and challenges to these examples. Acknowledging that there may be no perfect solution to a particular sustainability challenge should not deter us from trying to identify the most appropriate design response.

The aim of this book

The aim of this book is to examine the ways in which design and 'Sustainability' (with a big 'S') interrelate. We want to encourage a critically engaged application of design craft and design thinking to current and future societal challenges. At the heart of the book is the belief that design can drive considered changes in our society, and that design gives us the power to create the world we want to live in. Design thinking is increasingly being used to address our biggest societal challenges; as such design can be a powerful driver of action for sustainable change.

Design thinking is increasingly being used to address our biggest societal challenges; as such design can be a powerful driver of action for sustainable change.

About the authors

Paul's story

I've always been a generalist, hopefully in the best sense of the word. I'm not a designer, which is to say I haven't had formal design training. Neither have I been formally schooled in environmental sciences or politics. Nevertheless I now teach 'sustainability' to designers and work in what is now called Education for Sustainable Development (ESD). I am a professional communicator about/on sustainability, residing in a Faculty of Art, Design and Architecture.

My undergraduate studies were in philosophy, from which I gradually moved into the study of innovation, then into social research, then design research and then quite serendipitously into 'sustainability'. This all seems to make sense in retrospect, but was certainly not an intentional path. So many people now specializing in sustainability seem to have taken an equally indirect route.

My earliest exposure to design and designing was probably the same as for most other members of my generation: building toy Lego. I failed to inherit my father's obsession with classic cars, or his practical skills as a roofer. I found my obsession aged eight, in the form of guitars. Whether or not being a musician makes me a designer is a debate probably to be had elsewhere.

The biggest solo research project I've undertaken asked the question 'what is design?' a question I ask of all my student classes. In a way, this book is an opportunity for me to keep exploring that same question, and others. The sustainability agenda provides a great opportunity to ask the big questions about design itself (what? why? how?), which is why I like working at the point where the two connect.

To return to how I started this story, I often say that my specialism is generalism. The conversations that take place under the umbrella of 'sustainability', just as it relates to design, are hugely wide ranging. The role of the generalist is to make the connections that are invisible to the specialist, to synthesize as well as analyze; Victor Papanek wrote that in relation to designers in 1971, and it still resonates today.

I never studied 'sustainability' in the sense of being taught it. It is the nature of the field that while it is still emerging as a focus of academic study, it transcends established disciplines. Study of sustainability is self-reflexive, value-driven and increasingly, thankfully, inside the syllabus.

Anne's story

My interest in environmental issues began on walks with my father. He would take a large carrier bag with him on these walks and proceed to pick up litter and discuss local and national political issues, especially ones that had a real impact on those that were less fortunate or unable to look after themselves.

Throughout my school and college years I was involved in various environmental and animal rights pressure groups. When I arrived at London's Central Saint Martin's School of Art, on their undergraduate and postgraduate graphic design courses, I continued to pursue these interests. The connections between design, environmental deprivation and social injustice were encouraged during my design education but knowledge and guidance in this area were extremely limited.

As such I am totally self-taught in the area of design for sustainability and have always had a passion for providing learning opportunities for those who wish to become knowledgeable about design for sustainability topics.

This led me to write my first book, *The Graphic Designer's Greenbook* (Graphis, 1992). I have to acknowledge Michael Wolff (co-founder of Wolff Olins) who encouraged me to write this book and be part of a new wave of designers questioning the roles and responsibilities of designers. I'm still advocating design for sustainability to the design profession twenty years later, who still keep seeking clarification as well as information on this important topic. I have been blessed with postgraduate students who have been invaluable in 'kicking the tyres' on this book's ideas and contents and also continually expanding and challenging my knowledge and assumptions. That is the invaluable relationship between research and teaching.

I am currently Reader in Sustainable Design and Course Director of the MA Design for Development course at Kingston University, London as well as Adjunct Professor at the University of Calgary, Canada.

In addition, to writing journal papers, book chapters and undertaking funded research projects, I'm an advisor on various external initiatives such as the UK Design Museum's Sustainable Futures exhibition. In 2009 *Design Week* magazine identified me as one of the most influential advocates of sustainable design.

Paul Micklethwaite

Anne Chick

How to get
the most out of
this book

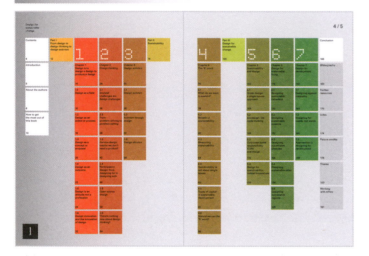

1 Structure

The table of contents reveals the
overall structure of the book,
consisting of seven chapters divided
into three colour-coded parts to aid
navigation.

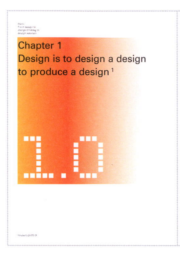

2 Chapters

Each chapter introduces a different
aspect of sustainability, design or
how they interlink, broken down
into sections and accompanied by
relevant photographs, diagrams
and quotations.

5 Quotations

Highlighted quotations provide
additional insight into the issues
being discussed.

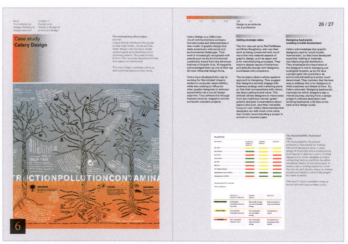

6 Case studies

The case studies in each chapter
illustrate the application of design for
sustainable change in different
real-world contexts.

3 Interviews

Within each chapter there are interviews with leading thinkers, academics and practitioners.

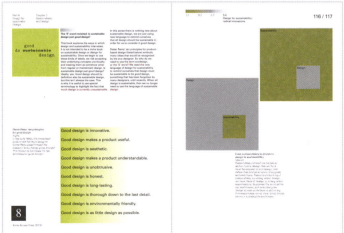

4 Photographs

Many of the subjects described in the book are illustrated by photographs supplied by leading practitioners.

7 Diagrams

Some of the more complex concepts of sustainable design are explained using simple diagrams.

8 Footnotes

Footnotes provide the author name, year of publication and page number where relevant, for the works cited in the text. Full details of the documents cited can be found in the bibliography on pages 168–169.

Part I
From design to design thinking to design activism

Design is increasingly recognized as a key element of the contemporary focus on the need for greater ecological and societal sustainability. Part I examines the various potential roles for design in this context, by first considering 'what is design?'

Design is traditionally discussed in terms of design disciplines and professions, and the industries they serve. Design thinking looks beyond these confines to suggest a wider role for design in addressing our biggest societal challenges. Design activism goes even further in suggesting more radical ways in which design can transform our society and the way we live, both now and for the future.

Part I
From design to
design thinking to
design activism

Chapter 1
Design is to design a design
to produce a design [1]

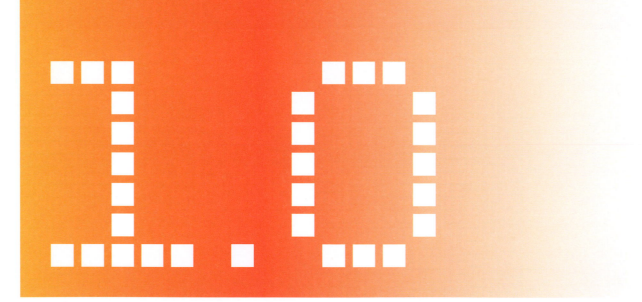

Part I
From design to
design thinking to
design activism

[1] Heskett (2005:3)

At first glance, the title of this chapter might not seem to make very much sense. Yet it uses the word 'design' in four very different, but useful, ways. First, design is a field or discipline. Second, design is an action or process. Third, a design is a concept, proposal or plan. Finally, the outcome of a design process is also called a 'design'. This chapter examines all these uses of the word 'design'. It then asks if design is in fact an attitude, rather than a profession, available to all of us? Case studies of two value-driven design consultancies help us to address this question. The chapter ends by considering the link between design and innovation and the extent to which design itself is changing.

Part I
From design to
design thinking to
design activism

Chapter 1
Design is to
design a design to
produce a design

1.1
Design as a field

The design sector [2]
(below)
Here, 'design' refers to a grouping of professional and commercial activities that contribute to a national economy. The design sector is now often located within the broader categorization of the 'creative industries', which are seen as key to the competitiveness of national economies.

Peripheral activities
— Manufacturing industry
— Modelling and prototype making
— Research and development within industry

Related industries
— Public relations
— Management consultancy
— Architecture

Related activities
— Fine art
— Graphic design
— Fashion design
— Crafts (e.g. small-scale furniture makers)
— Multimedia design

Core activities
— Design consultancies
— The design component of industry

[2] Buchanan (1992:9–10)

Design is a field or discipline. Design in this sense is aligned to our material and visual culture, it relates directly to the artefacts and products of our human-made cultures. The field of design can be explored in a number of ways.

Design history

Design history is the broad academic discipline investigating the function, form and materials of artefacts of the pre-industrial and industrial periods, up to and including the present day. It focuses on artefacts' production, dissemination and consumption as well as their cultural, economic and social meanings.

Design studies

The emerging field of design studies examines design and its role in society from a broad range of critical perspectives. It considers design from the perspective of disciplines such as history, philosophy and sociology. Design studies focuses on contemporary design practice and culture, and explores the 'what?' and 'why?', as well as the 'how?', of design and designing.

The design industry

Design can also be used in this sense to indicate an industry or set of professions, as in 'the design industry', or 'the design professions'. You've used the word in this way if you've ever said 'I want to work in design'. Government also talks about design in this way when it discusses the importance of design to the economy. Here, design is a grouping of professional and commercial activities. A business also talks about design in this way when it describes itself as being 'design-led'.

Design management

The discipline and profession of design management is concerned with the management of design strategies, processes and projects. We might also say that design management focuses on the effective strategic exploitation of design for commercial gain, as design is increasingly seen as a primary strategic asset for any organization.

Design and art

Design is often considered in relation to art, and the two fields certainly overlap. Art puts a primary emphasis on self-expression; it is a creative activity whose origin and motivation is personal to the individual. Design is based not on self-expression but on discovering a problem shared by many people and trying to solve it. Design is inherently constrained by the demands of a client, a brief or a market. Design, therefore, represents a different type of creative activity to art. Design has in fact been known as 'applied art' and 'commercial art' at different points in its history.

Design and craft

Design can also be considered in relation to craft. Craft production is usually based on traditional, skilled manual labour and produces artefacts in small numbers. Design is generally aligned with mass manufacture, however designer-makers design and make their products to bring together their creative ideas and making skills in individual or batch productions of their designs. This approach is attractive to those designers seeking an alternative to mass-production orthodoxies.

Categorizing design

The field of design is often sub-divided into further categories. We might talk of broad areas in which design is explored by professional designers and also by non-designers. These design areas are defined in terms of the nature of the design outcome, the type of thing that is designed. Ways of categorizing design outcomes are explored on pages 22–23.

Categories of design

1 Symbolic and visual communications.

2 Material objects.

3 Activities and organized services.

4 Complex systems or environments for living, working, playing, and learning.[3]

[3] Department for Culture, Media and Sport, UK (1998:35)

Part I
From design to
design thinking to
design activism

Chapter 1
Design is to
design a design to
produce a design

1.2
Design as an action or process

Design is also a verb describing an action or process. We use 'design' in this way when we talk about 'designing'. Designers have fought hard to gain recognition for what they do as being more than mere styling or decoration.

Historically, design was at the end of the business or product development process. Product designers, for example, have often been confined to providing a shell for a new piece of technology developed by engineers. Design is increasingly seen as a more fundamental process concerned with the creative conceptualization of our communications, products, systems and societal structures.

We're all designers?

It is sometimes said that *everyone* is a designer. The planning and patterning of our actions towards a desired result constitutes designing. In this sense, everyone who devises courses of action aimed at changing existing situations into preferred ones can be said to be designing.

Three design process models
(right)
The act of designing is sometimes formalized in a design process model. There are many representations of the design process, reflecting the many ways there are of designing. These models of design process often appear to have little in common with each other. Rather than thinking of design as a single process that we all follow in the same way, we might think that every designer has their own process that is personal to them. Models are abstractions of reality; how accurate can a design process model actually be in depicting designing?

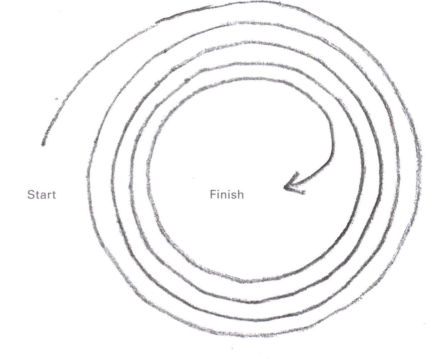

Start   Finish

So we are designing when we follow a recipe, when we compose a piece of music, even when we decide what to wear in the morning (we're designing our 'look' for the day). This universal sense of designing, in which we are *all* designers, is sometimes thought of as one of the fundamental characteristics that make us human.

What are the limits of this broad idea of designing? Some writers think that writing or talking about design is a form of designing, because by discussing design we are in effect 'designing design'; that is, defining and redefining the field of design (see pages 24–25).

Design process models

The act of designing is sometimes formalized in a design process model, but who are these design process models for? Do designers use them? Often not.

Are they devised by theorists trying to demystify or explain an activity (designing), which is beyond analysis? Or are these models developed by designers in response to an expectation, perhaps from their clients, that they do use a model?

A key aspect of the idea of design as an activity or process is that we learn how to do it. We may have an aptitude for designing, but we develop our capability for designing through experience and, often, formal design training and education. The extent to which designers are 'born or made' is up for discussion. Like a self-taught or instinctual musician who is afraid to analyze too closely what he or she does, for fear of losing their apparently mysterious musical ability, some designers are reluctant to delve into the process of their designing too deeply. It might, of course, suit professional designers to maintain that designing is the preserve of a 'chosen few'! The opposing view is that designers don't own designing and that design capability, like creativity, is potentially inherent in everyone, everywhere.

Design is values made visible

Designing is also a culturally bound activity. While we may think of a particular designer, perhaps even ourselves, as having a gift for designing, it is certainly the case that our influences and values are expressed when we design. In this sense, no one designs in a vacuum, design always reflects the context in which it takes place. Design is 'values made visible', where those values are both personal and collective.

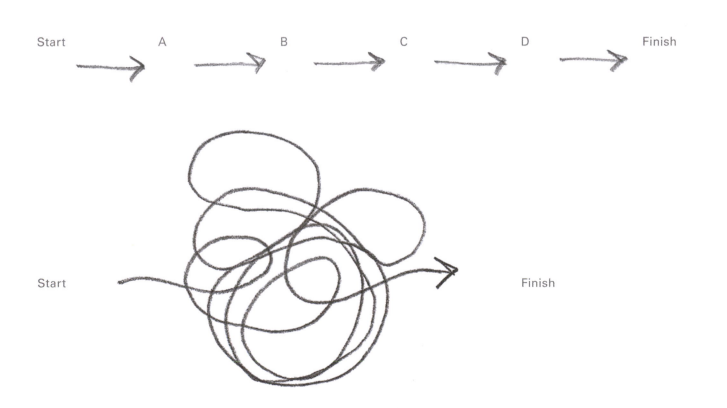

Part I
From design to
design thinking to
design activism

Chapter 1
Design is to
design a design to
produce a design

1.3
Design as a concept
or proposal

Design is also a noun meaning 'a concept, proposal or plan'. Design can be defined as our ability to prefigure what we create before we create it. This is one way in which design differs from craft; the craftsperson often does not know the outcome of the making process when they begin. Instead, the craftsperson explores and experiments through making. The designer, on the other hand, knows the outcome of the production process before it starts; the designer's work is done prior to manufacture. The outcome of this process of 'prefiguring' is a concept, proposal or plan, which is then produced or manufactured.

Design models

This definition of design derives from the way in which a Renaissance painter would first sketch out an outline of his composition before committing valuable materials to the realization of the painting. A design model, for example, serves the same function. Materials are valuable, and it is easier to make changes to a design before we commit resources to realizing it in tangible form.

Modelling is also useful because we may be less inclined to make changes to, and take risks with, something we have begun to build in the real world. The early phase of design is a form of play as we experiment with possibilities that still only exist on paper, in foam or in a virtual environment. Once this phase is complete, we might build a more refined model that functions as a prototype, for eliciting user needs or testing in terms of technical or user feasibility.

Degree of realization

A design proposal suggests an intervention in a scenario or context with a view to bringing an improvement. As such, the design concept needs to be realized to an extent that is sufficient to convince a client, user or consumer (and also the designer) that it can work.

A design proposal may go through much iteration, from a rough sketch to a detailed blueprint for automated manufacture.

Design concept sketch
(below)
A design concept or proposal can be
expressed as a basic sketch. Even very
complex design concepts, such as a
bridge or skyscraper, can initially be
shown in very crude terms. The iconic
shape of Norman Foster's completed
'Gherkin' office building in London is
apparent even in this early sketch.

a reflective
solar top
following
the 'o'
shading...

The
'maypole'
effect?

The
city
grid

The "city grid" is
really av 4 storey
increment, visually

The "city within a city" has
always been full of surprises!

Part I
From design to
design thinking to
design activism

Chapter 1
Design is to
design a design to
produce a design

1.4
Design as an outcome

The Freeplay Indigo Lantern
(below and right)
A design outcome is an embodiment
or realization of a design concept.
A manufactured product like this wind-
up lantern is a physical design outcome.
The detailed design specification
('blueprint') used for its manufacture
can also be considered to be a design
outcome, albeit one that is less tangible
and used as a means of creating
something physical.

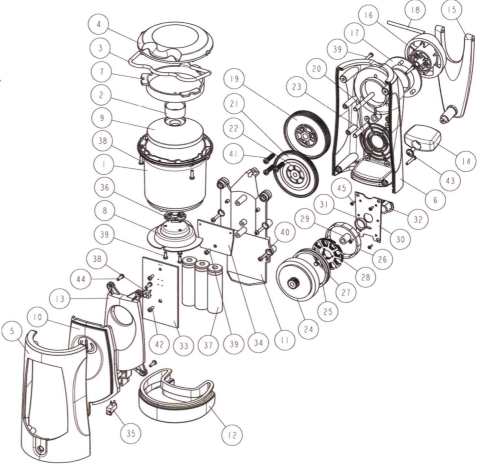

The outcomes of designing (perhaps formalized in a design process) can take a wide range of forms and scales – from a pasta shape, to a building, to an urban plan. It's also worth bearing in mind that design outcomes (the things we design) are not necessarily physical or tangible.

In each categorization (see the 'Design outcomes' box below) there is a progression from very concrete outcomes to outcomes that are more intangible. The maturing of design as a profession is reflected in the growing ambition of designers in applying their design capabilities on ever larger scales. An increasing range of outcomes can be seen as the fruit of a conscious application of 'design thinking'.

Service design

An example of the growing ambition of designers in identifying where they can usefully intervene is the emergence of the specialism of service design. This is a mode of designing characterized by the creation of services, rather than simply products.

Physical products can be viewed as the means by which services are delivered, and at the heart of service delivery is an experience. While a service may seem intangible in itself, it will incorporate a number of 'touchpoints', all of which involve conventional tangible design outcomes. Service design therefore includes the creation of many other forms of design outcome.

Design is a political act

Therefore design suggests an intervention in a scenario or context with a view to bringing an improvement. As such, all designing is political. Guy Bonsieppe's notion of 'political' was 'the citizen contributing to a broad political dialogue within society, where the question being asked is "in what sort of society do we want to live?" rather than a narrow view of party politics'. [4] This can be clearly seen in the categorizations given in the 'Design outcomes' box below.

The design of 'futures' and opinions has far-reaching consequences not only for our material world (what we make and how we make it) but also for our mental life (how we think about the world and our place within it). The more ambitious the nature of a design outcome, the more responsibility we have to consider the implications of the change it might entail.

Design outcomes		Many different categorizations of design outcomes have been proposed, varying in complexity:
1	**2**	**3**
Things	**Objects**	**Products** Objects, things, industrial design, ergonomics, consumer goods
Places	**Communications**	**Capital goods** Means of production of consumer goods, production machinery
Messages[5]	**Environments**	**Buildings** Architecture, physical structures
	Identities	**Urban areas** City planning, built environment
	Systems	**Transportation** Networks and infrastructures
	Contexts	**Communication systems** Telephone networks, 'virtual' systems and networks
	Futures[6]	**Institutions** Hierarchical and functional structures
		Festivities Events, temporal design
		Markets, public services, laws Codes for and means of living
		Processes Methodologies, ways of working and doing
		Opinions Philosophies, ways of seeing [7]

[5] Norman (2008)   [6] Heskett (2005)   [7] Jones (1992)

Part I
From design to
design thinking to
design activism

Chapter 1
Design is to
design a design to
produce a design

1.5
Design is an attitude not a profession

There is increasing debate in design courses, magazines and websites as to whether the act of designing should be seen not just as a profession, which is sanctioned by paying clients, but as an attitude. Put simply, an 'attitude' is a collection of values and beliefs around a certain subject, held by an individual, which makes them act and react in certain ways. Viewing design as an attitude, rather than just a profession, gives designers the responsibility to ask what kind of designer they wish to be. This is not a new concept but, unfortunately, it is still a novel one. Design thinkers such as Richard Buckminster Fuller, László Moholy-Nagy, Victor Papanek and Norman Potter debated this issue throughout the twentieth century.

The scope of design

For far too long, the design community has viewed political, social and environmental concerns as being beyond its remit. This status quo has been upheld by a design education system primarily concerned with training future designers for the business of designing and selling 'stuff'.

Design thinking and design craft

What is the difference between design thinking and design craft?

Design thinking is the ability to apply creativity to the formulation and resolution of problems and challenges.

Design craft is the ability to translate this design thinking into design outcomes, either tangible (such as a product) or intangible (such as a service or way of working). Design thinking is a capability we all have to varying extents.

We only acquire design craft through training and practice, such as traditionally delivered by design schools. So we might say that while anyone *can* be a designer, not everyone *is* a designer in the sense of being able to apply 'designerly' ways of thinking to the generation of actual design outcomes. To do that, we need design training and a different set of aptitudes and skills.

1.1   1.2   1.3   1.4   1.5   1.6

1.5
Design is an attitude
not a profession

24 / 25

Design has been downgraded from being fundamentally engaged with an understanding of ideas, and a powerful tool for social change, to the learning of often mundane technical capabilities.

This situation is beginning to be questioned by a new breed of young, determined, creative idealists who want to harness both design craft and design thinking as levers for political and societal change. New perspectives, ideas and technologies are being harnessed to push designing beyond being just a tool for business.

When we are surrounded by problems and challenges, design presents a positive approach to generating ideas, connections and solutions. This is evident in websites and forums such as www.treehugger.com. It is also evident in ideologically led design exhibitions such as the Cooper-Hewitt National Design Museum's *Designing for the Other 90%* (2007) (see pages 154–155) and the British Design Museum's *Sustainable Futures* (2010). The Society for Responsible Design's annual *Change* exhibition showcases the directions that graduates from top Australian universities see the world taking. Previous student exhibitors have become Australian Design Award finalists, with some designs receiving global exposure.

Design does not belong to designers

Traditionally, the design industry has been the domain of self-appointed professionals with a recognized art or design school education. Status as a professional designer was based on a formal design training. This is changing as increasing numbers of professionals without a traditional design education are working in the design industries. You don't necessarily have to be a designer or to have undergone design training to work in the design sector.

Designers have never had the same professional status as, for example, architects, who must undergo an approved training programme before they qualify and begin practising professionally. Design has never had that degree of professional protection, and so we see increasing numbers of design professionals who are not professional designers in the traditional sense. Design companies may be headed by people who have no formal design training, but who do have wider experience that they bring to bear on the management and application of design to real-world challenges.

These non-designing champions will, of course, lead teams of traditional designers in the translation of design thinking into specific design outcomes through the application of design craft. So we might say that while designing still belongs to designers, design itself does not.

The broadening engagement in professional design can be seen as a sign of design's increasing maturity as a sector. Design is strengthened by the involvement of professionals from beyond the traditional art and design school. Fields such as psychology, sociology and ethnography have much to contribute to the effective application of design to our growing shared societal challenges, and they bring expertise that is not necessarily to be found in designers themselves. Those with training and expertise in these other disciplines can help to direct collective design thinking in the best direction. It is then generally for designers themselves to implement this design thinking in the most successful ways possible.

"The idea of design and the profession of the designer has to be transformed from the notion of a specialist function into a generally valid attitude of resourcefulness and inventiveness which allows projects to be seen not in isolation but in relationship with the need of the individual and the community. One cannot simply lift out any subject matter from the complexity of life and try to handle it as an independent unit."

László Moholy-Nagy
Vision in Motion, (1947:42)

Part I
From design to
design thinking to
design activism

Chapter 1
Design is to
design a design to
produce a design

Case study
Celery Design

The ecological guide to paper
(below)
Celery Design developed this guide
to help their studio, clients and the
wider design community to weigh
up ecological considerations when
choosing papers. The guide directs
them to the very best recycled and tree-
free papers on the market.

This tool is freely available online at
www.celerydesign.com/eco-tools.

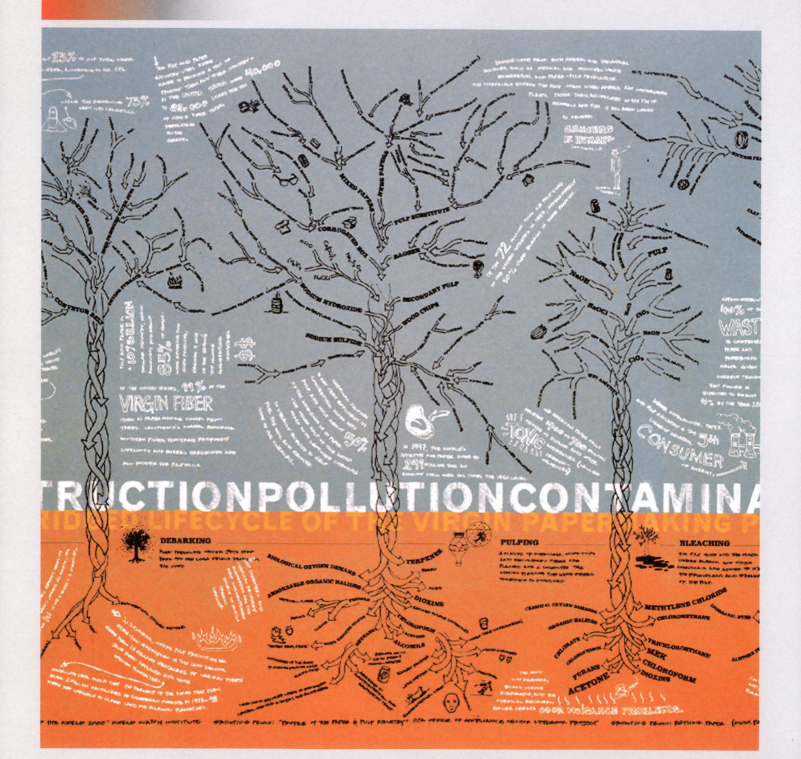

1.1 1.2 1.3 1.4 1.5 1.6
Design is an attitude
not a profession

26 / 27

Celery Design is a Californian visual communications company that advocates and demonstrates a new model of graphic design that deals proactively with social and environmental challenges. Their work is increasingly recognized with awards such as the Environmental Leadership Award from the American Institute of Graphic Arts. *ID* magazine acknowledged them as one of their top 40 most influential design firms.

Celery have developed this role by working for like-minded industry leaders in corporate responsibility, while also seeking to influence other graphic designers to embrace sustainability as a crucial design objective. They achieve this through frequent lectures, magazine articles and public outreach projects.

Adding strategic value

The firm was set up by Rod DeWeese and Brian Dougherty, who see their work as being concerned with much more than the material aspects of graphic design, such as paper and print manufacturing processes. They explore deeper issues of behaviour- and attitude-change with designers, businesses and consumers.

The company takes a whole-systems approach to designing. They suggest that designers actively engage with business strategy and marketing plans, so that their conversations with clients are about adding brand value. This attitude allows designers to move away from the traditional narrow 'green' graphic designer conversations about papers and print, and their inevitable focus on cost. Celery demonstrates that designers can add much more value than simply recommending a project is printed on recycled paper.

Designing backwards: avoiding trouble downstream

Celery acknowledges that graphic designers need to 'avoid trouble downstream', so they have developed expertise relating to materials, manufacturing and distribution. They emphasize the importance of the designer's role in managing-out ecological impacts, as by the time a project gets into production its environmental destiny is pretty much determined. They maintain that the best way to address this is for designers to think creatively and ahead-of-time. So, Celery advocate 'designing backwards', a process by which designers take a mental journey, starting from a design project's ultimate destination and working backwards until they arrive back at the design studio.

The Sustainability Scorecard
(left)
The Sustainability Scorecard provides a framework for making informed decisions about a wide range of materials and manufacturing techniques in relation to print. It helps designers to easily visualize multiple competing factors and filter the often simplistic claims of manufacturers. It uses a colour coding system to show the source and toxicity impacts, energy impact and destiny (end-of-life stage) for each material.

This tool is freely available online at www.celerydesign.com/eco-tools.

PLASTICS

MATERIAL	SOURCE & TOXICITY IMPACTS	ENERGY IMPACT	DESTINY
#1 PET	CAUTION	CAUTION	CAUTION
#2 HDPE	PREFERRED	CAUTION	CAUTION
#3 PVC	AVOID	CAUTION	AVOID
#4 LDPE	PREFERRED	CAUTION	AVOID
#5 PP	PREFERRED	CAUTION	AVOID
#6 PS	AVOID	CAUTION	AVOID
#7 Other Plastics	AVOID	CAUTION	AVOID
Biopolymers (non-GMO)	PREFERRED	PREFERRED	PREFERRED
Biopolymers (GMO)	AVOID	PREFERRED	PREFERRED

Perfect bind (PVA cold set)

Starch adhesive

	SOURCE & TOXICITY IMPACTS	ENERGY IMPACT	DESTINY
 PREFERRED	Sustainable renewable resource, non-toxic	Renewable energy, very low embodied energy	Fully recyclable or fully compostable
CAUTION	Conventional renewable resource	Non-renewable, low embodied energy	Incineration or mixed
AVOID	Non-renewable resource, toxic	Non-renewable, high embodied energy	Conventional or hazardous waste landfill

Part I
From design to
design thinking to
design activism

Chapter 1
Design is to
design a design to
produce a design

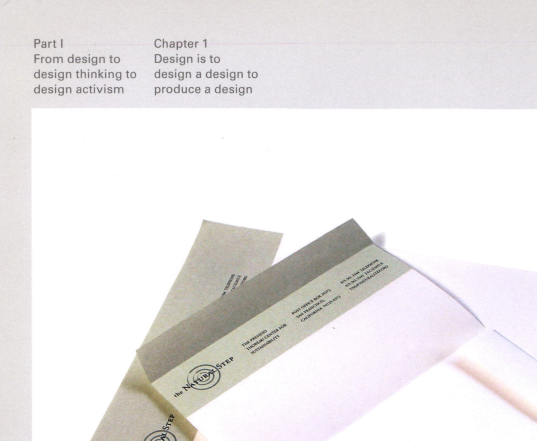

**Is it a letterhead or an envelope?
It's both**
(above)
Celery designed a comprehensive
identity for The Natural Step, a
non-profit research, education and
advisory group that helps corporations
and communities move towards
sustainability. The letterhead is
perforated and scored for easy self-
mailing, which eliminates the need for
most envelopes.

1.1 1.2 1.3 1.4 1.5 1.6
Design is an attitude
not a profession

28 / 29

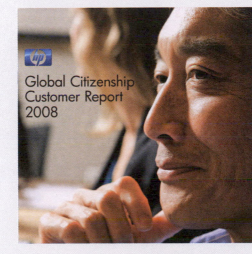

Hewlett Packard (HP) communicating its innovative corporate responsibility practices
(above)
Over the last five years, Celery has gradually shifted HP's corporate responsibility report from a single large document to a sophisticated web publishing model. This approach has reduced the printed material from more than 100 pages to 24 and created a family of targeted multimedia communications. Celery's collaboration with HP has enjoyed widespread recognition, including the Ceres Award for Outstanding Sustainability Report.

Elephant Pharmacy designs
(above)
The Elephant Pharmacy chain focuses on natural health and wellness. Celery's designs aim to appeal to an audience beyond the 'Berkeley hippy' stereotype. The hanging signs are made with bamboo plywood and the wall signs are laser-cut plywood with a natural stain. The banners are also made from recycled polyethylene using a printing technique with no solvent emissions.

Chocolatl packaging: a no-holds-barred eco-solution
(above)
This Celery packaging design comprises 100 per cent recycled paperboard box, compostable inner biopolymer bag, no glue, is efficient on the press sheet and is reversible for reuse as a gift box.

Part I
From design to
design thinking to
design activism

Chapter 1
Design is to
design a design to
produce a design

Interview
Joshua Blackburn

Joshua Blackburn
Founder of UK-based communications
agency Provokateur

What's your background?

I'm not a designer. I studied Social and
Political Sciences in the early 1990s. I
founded the ethical communications
agency Provokateur in 2002. I learnt
the power of design and how to craft
effective strategic communications in
the social and political spheres working
on the 1997 UK general election under
Tony Blair's strategy adviser Philip
Gould. I wanted to know more about
how to create effective communications
campaigns, so I moved on to leading
global brand consultancy Wolff Olins
where I worked as their specialist in
not-for-profit clients. This was from
choice, as I didn't want to work on
their corporate accounts. I learnt how
powerful advertising, branding and
design are to changing attitudes and
behaviours.

I write a lot in the (UK) national press
and on the Web as well as speaking
at conferences, generally agitating on
numerous issues such as 'can design
help save the world?'

Why did you set up Provokateur?

My ambition was to create a new kind of
agency that would transform the world
of ethical communications. I wanted
to set up an agency that did work that
redefines the rules. Provokateur use
the tools of advertising and branding,
but apply these commercially proven
methods to clients with social and
ideological agendas. One thing that
advertising people know well is the
power of seduction. They recognized
long ago that the way to the head is
via the heart, and use every device of
charm, delight and aesthetic allure to
get there. Ethical communications need
the same force of attraction.

As Provokateur's manifesto declares,
'we hold an unreasonable belief that
you can change the world'. We work
only with clients we believe in, which
is generally a host of environmental,
charitable and cultural organizations.
We do work for companies, but only
ones we like.

We Want Tap
(left)
Think globally – drink locally –
drink responsibly – get on tap

Setting up Provokateur has allowed me to instigate our own campaigns, too. We don't have to wait around for an organization to commission us. Our commitment to being an 'agency for change' is reflected in our self-funded enterprises. Our biggest ventures to date are the *Acme Climate Action* book and 'We Want Tap' campaign. We fund, create and launch these self-initiated projects ourselves.

What was the idea behind We Want Tap?

The objective of the We Want Tap campaign was to get people to drink tap water rather than bottled mineral water via a stylish, seductive campaign that would reveal the truth about bottled water and bust the myths about tap.

Bottled water is one consumer product that bears little scrutiny. It consumes precious resources, produces mountains of rubbish, costs a fortune – and all the while drinking water comes out of our taps for free in the UK and many other countries. Bottled water is the triumph of marketing over common sense. To change people's behaviour, the campaign produced 'Tap' products, such as a reusable water bottle and Do-It-Yourself Bottled Water Kit. Profits from sales went towards water projects in the developing world. The campaign really caught the imagination, attracting heaps of press attention and got people talking. It won Best Integrated Campaign at the 2008 Green Awards. We are presently re-vamping the Tap bottle with a Tom Dixon design and taking the campaign to the next level.

And what about the Acme Climate Action campaign?

Acme Climate Action is another self-generated project, but one that uses a different box of design tricks. We worked with the publisher to produce an 'interactive book' stuffed with ways of getting the message out there that everyone's actions make a difference to climate change. It's less a book, more a loosely bound folder of projects and prompts. It's designed to be taken apart and utilized. It has stickers for your light switches and home appliances, letters to send to politicians and companies, a home energy audit, labels to reuse your envelopes, postcards to spread the word and loads more. Even the front and back cover are designed to be made into a picture frame. The book is meant to be fun. We believe strongly in utilizing humour to communicate such a serious topic.

Acme Climate Action book
(left)
The *Acme Climate Action* book is one of Provokateur's self-initiated projects which they fund, create and launch themselves. Humour is used to great effect on the serious subject of climate change.

Part I
From design to
design thinking to
design activism

Chapter 1
Design is to
design a design to
produce a design

1.6
Design innovation and the innovation of design

The designer is 'T-shaped'
(below)
A designer can be described as being
'T-shaped', where the horizontal bar of
the 'T' represents generalist knowledge
and breadth of expertise, and the
vertical stem represents specialist
knowledge and depth of expertise.

Breadth of expertise

Depth of expertise

Specialist

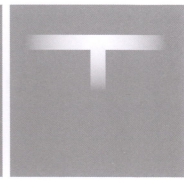

Generalist

Design is considered by many to be key to innovation, which is in turn considered to be key to economic competitiveness. Policy makers and leading companies alike are committed to design-led innovation, particularly in the so-called creative industries.

Design is also increasingly seen as a key factor in *social* innovation; that is, innovation that delivers benefits that are not quantifiable solely (or perhaps even partially) in financial terms. Design is a tool for making changes in the world. We should, therefore, keep asking ourselves what (and who) is design for? We should keep innovating design itself.

Specialism and generalism

Increased recognition of the value of design raises the issue of who does design, and how? The profile of any individual designer can be represented in terms of relative degrees of specialism and generalism. The designer is 'T-shaped' (see diagram opposite), where the horizontal bar of the 'T' represents *generalist* knowledge and expertise, and the vertical stem of the 'T' represents *specialist* knowledge and expertise.

Specialist expertise is clearly important, yet we should not undervalue the ability to synthesize and integrate specialist expertise with wider over-arching perspectives. An emphasis on professionalization can undervalue the often valuable contribution of the non-professional and the amateur (in the best sense of the word). The individual designer can't hope to be capable in all areas, and so must collaborate in interdisciplinary teams. Wisdom, unlike expertise, is collective rather than individual.

Design participation

It can be argued that design is the most powerful tool we have to transform our society and the way we live, both now and for the future. As such, design is for all of us. There is an increasing recognition that design should not be the preserve of the few acting on our behalf, but that we all have a role to play in using the power of design to shape and reshape our world. This democratization of design can be seen in the gradual shift in the way it is talked about and the way it is done. Perhaps we can not yet say that 'we are all designers now', but a shift is taking place from the passive consumption of, to a more active participation in, design.

New roles for designers

As design is no longer seen as the exclusive preserve of the professional designer, new roles for designers are emerging. Design is now seen as being too important to be left to the designer alone. We are seeing an opening-up of the practice of design as, through co-design and participatory design approaches, people (not 'users' or 'consumers') are being involved in the creation of their own design outcomes. New roles are constantly emerging as the designer becomes less a generator of ideas and more a facilitator of the generation of ideas.

"Innovation is the successful exploitation of new ideas."

Department of Trade and Industry
Competing in the Global Economy: The Innovation Challenge, UK (2003:8)

Part I
From design to
design thinking to
design activism

Chapter 2
Design thinking

'Design' is usually discussed in relation to particular design disciplines and professions, along with the industries which they serve. Does this traditional view capture all that design is and does? The emerging concept of 'design thinking' looks beyond the confines of the design professions and designer-client relationships to suggest a wider role for design in addressing our biggest societal challenges. Design is not just about solving problems; it can also be about problem-finding. Design and designers can redefine problems to arrive at better solutions and outcomes.

A design outcome may not always be a physical, tangible product. It may be a service or a new way of doing things. In some cases, we may not need a new product, just a better way of integrating the products we already have in order to serve our needs. Design is also too important, and too useful, to be used only by professional designers. The active participation of users in the design process can ensure more successful design outcomes. The emergence of open-source design is creating a collaborative remix culture in which the originator of an idea passes it on to others to take in new directions.

But is design thinking really anything new, or is it just a case of the emperor's new clothes?

Part I
From design to
design thinking to
design activism

Chapter 2
Design thinking

2.1
Societal challenges are design challenges

"Today we have the opportunity… [to] unleash the power of design thinking as a means of exploring new possibilities, creating new choices, and bringing new solutions to the world. In the process, we may find that we have made our societies healthier, our businesses more profitable, and our own lives richer and more meaningful."

Tim Brown
*Change by Design: How Design
Thinking Transforms Organizations and
Inspires Innovation,* (2009:230)

This book is about how design is evolving and how it is now being applied to a much wider spectrum of social and environmental issues through a new design thinking agenda. Design is going through a period of intellectual expansion, and adapting to participate in new arenas beyond its usual professional territories. This is resulting in designers themselves evolving and developing greater 'design mindfulness' (in John Thackara's phrase[1]) in relation to *what* they do, what they can do and *how* they do it. With this broadening scope for designers has come the view that design thinking is not the sole domain of the professional design community.

Design, in the form of design thinking, is increasingly seen as embodying a set of principles that can be applied by a diverse range of people to a wide range of challenges.

Transformation design: designing in new contexts

The UK Design Council has been exploring this area for a decade, during which time they have pioneered the concept of transformation design. The core idea of transformation design is that the design process can be applied to almost any problem.

It is specifically concerned with applying design skills in non-traditional territories such as public services. These new settings for design can be thought of as non-commercial, in either the public sector or the so-called 'third' (voluntary and not-for-profit) sector. This is design in the public rather than the commercial realm.

A new design discipline?

If societal challenges are design challenges, how does this reframe design itself? Advocates of transformation design claim that they are involved in the creation of a new design discipline; one which applies and develops traditional design skills to directly address social issues. But does this focus on bigger societal issues justify talk of a new design discipline? What has changed here? Are we seeing new design values, new design methods, or perhaps both?

Transformation design asks designers to shape behaviour – of people, systems and organizations – as well as form. As such, its outcomes are often intangible, and certainly not confined to the traditional notion of a designed artefact. It asks us to accept an organization as being a designed object.

So the contexts and outcomes of transformation design are new. Does it also involve a new design methodology? Is it done differently to conventional design?

Transformation design projects have the following six characteristics:

1 Defining and redefining the brief.

2 Collaborating between disciplines.

3 Employing participatory design techniques.

4 Building capacity, not dependency.

5 Designing beyond traditional solutions.

6 Creating fundamental change.[2]

Transformation design has participatory design principles and methods at its core. We'll explore participatory design more fully later in this chapter (see pages 46–49).

[1] Thackara (2005:226)

[2] Cottam et al (2006:20–22)

Part I
From design to
design thinking to
design activism

Chapter 2
Design thinking

2.2
From problem-solving to problem-setting

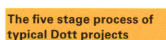

The five stage process of typical Dott projects

1
Diagnose phase
Setting up the project, and diagnosing the nature of the problem, including:
— Identifying existing research and activity happening around the issue.
— Bringing together a co-design team.
— Building a picture of the existing services, expertise and best practice.
— Sharpening the brief toward a more focused issue that is closely aligned to the community.

2
Co-discovery phase
This stage researches with the wider community the local issue. The design teams work with user groups, particularly local communities, and a wider stakeholder group including service providers and other experts. They use a range of well-known and emergent design tools such as observation, cultural probes, design ethnography and user diaries.

The ideas behind design thinking emerged from methods that are common to nearly all design fields, be it industrial, graphic, interior or any other design profession. These basic operating principles constitute a process that might be expressed most simply as: the way that designers approach problems and achieve solutions. Designers often think of themselves as problem-solvers rather than problem-finders. Successful design outcomes, however, come from a deep understanding of the problem requiring solution, even to the extent of reframing the problem itself.

The most successful designers attempt to uncover the assumptions in a given statement of a problem, and to explore new ways of thinking about the problem itself.

What is design thinking?

Tim Brown, Chief Executive of IDEO and a high-profile advocate of design thinking, has commented that the power of design is not just as a link in a chain but as the hub of a wheel. He uses the term 'design thinking' as a way of describing a set of principles that can be applied by diverse people to a wide range of problems. These principles turn out to be applicable to a wide range of organizations, not just to companies in search of new products.

A competent designer can always improve upon last year's new product or visual communication, but Brown argues that an interdisciplinary team of skilled design thinkers is in a position to tackle more complex problems. From health care systems to obesity, and crime prevention to climate change, design thinking is now being applied to a wide range of challenges.

Others argue that the best and most important part of design is the doing, not the thinking, and that a focus on design thinking over design practice undervalues what designers actually bring to a project. Nevertheless, there is growing consensus that design provides a set of skills, tools and methods that can guide people to new solutions and address large-scale social challenges in the private, public and third (voluntary and not-for-profit) sectors.

The Design Council in the UK has embraced design thinking and service design and moved designers and design into addressing issues in the public sector and communities. The council describes this process as a sequence of steps that defines problems, discovers solutions and makes them real. Through the Dott projects (see pages 140–141) they have developed collaborative design methods and processes (often referred to as 'participatory design') to work with communities to design and develop new solutions to local issues. They work with design agencies such as Engine (see pages 48–49) who bring innovation and human-centered methods to the projects. See pages 46–47 for further details on participatory design.

3
Co-design phase
Co-designing is where the team and/or community are involved in idea generation with professional designers and other experts. The design team uses the research with local people in the co-discovery phase to generate new ideas and innovation.
Then the co-design stage is built upon to create tangible aspects that can be communicated and prototyped with the community, including:
— Building on ideas, moving from sketches to formalized visualizations.
— Prototyping of ideas (which can be 'low fidelity' mock ups or working prototypes).
— Gathering feedback from local people on improving ideas before implementation.

4
Co-delivery
Outputs and outcomes at this stage vary. Dott projects typically create innovative ways that people can engage with the design solution in the medium or longer term, including:
— Transferring ownership of the project to the community.
— Ensuring project management skills are in place for implementation.
— Scaling the project or business planning.
— Ongoing design changes.

5
Legacy
Legacies can include the visible outputs from the projects or also embedded legacies such as:
— The thinking, ideas and practices that reside in, remain and continue being used by the individuals who participated on the projects.
— Participants who become champions for design, sharing new approaches of thinking and doing in their organizations and communities.

The Design Council emphasize that the embedded legacies are not highly visible and usually manifest themselves in other ideas and areas that may or may not be related to the Dott project. More information can be found at www.designcouncil.org.uk

Part I
From design to
design thinking to
design activism

Chapter 2
Design thinking

Case study
Flowmaker

There are several design inspiration tools that seek to open up creative problem-setting and problem-solving through the application of design thinking. These tools aim to generate new views on a design challenge, to inspire creativity and to support communication and collaboration within a design team (which may not necessarily include just designers). These design inspiration tools help us to explore a design challenge, to perhaps reframe it, and to evaluate and select the best research methods for the job. Above all, these tools encourage a human-centred and empathic approach to the design process, with a view to generating better and more relevant design outcomes.

2.1   **2.2**   2.3   2.4   2.5   2.6
From problem-solving
to problem-setting

40 / 41

Design creativity cards

Based on the familiar pack of playing cards, the Flowmaker pack consists of 58 cards in five colour-coded suits (instinct, personality, ageing, play and potential), each relating to a particular area of focus:

— **Instinct** (blue) explores 'design to fulfil needs'.

— **Personality** (green) explores 'design for others'.

— **Ageing** (yellow) explores 'design for our future selves'.

— **Play** (orange) explores 'design for joy and interaction'.

— **Potential** (red) explores 'design for sustainability' (deliberately not colour-coded as the green suit).

The Flowmaker cards can be used to enhance the design process in a huge variety of ways:

1   **Create a random brief**
Pick a card from each suit to generate a new scenario to design for.

2   **Define a brief**
Use specific cards to develop or tighten an existing design brief.

3   **Create a user profile**
Select cards to define a particular user to design for.

4   **Idea generation**
Pick a card at random as an aid to brainstorming.

5   **Group brainstorms**
Deal cards to encourage design participants to consider an issue from new angles.

6   **Evaluating projects**
Critique an existing design solution using selected cards.

Flowmaker, as its name suggests, is intended to be an open-ended, multi-purpose, user-adaptable aid to the design process; it does not have a single prescriptive methodology. Users of Flowmaker are given just enough information and guidance to get them started, and are then encouraged to find the best ways of using the tool to release their own collective creativity. Each project could potentially generate a new method, insofar as each design project is individual and has its own priorities. Flowmaker's creators, WEmake, use the tool themselves in sessions with corporate clients and in educational settings, as well as in their own design consultancy and self-initiated projects.

Exercise can help maintain the muscles needed for balance and co-ordination and reduce the risk of falls.

BALANCE

Choosing to surrender to uncontrollable events.

CHANCE

Is an object necessary? Can you use something that already exists? Is your design a service?

DEMATERIALISE

Responding to danger or discomfort by running away, escaping (physically or mentally).

FLIGHT

Jill / Jack of all trades, pursues a broad range of activities that have a low entry threshold.

GENERALIST

Dizziness, light-headedness, rush, vertigo.

HEAD SPIN

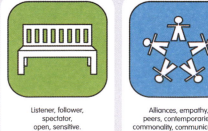

Listener, follower, spectator, open, sensitive.

RECEPTIVE

Alliances, empathy, peers, contemporaries, commonality, communication, mutual support.

SOCIAL - FRIENDS

Aerobic, muscular and skeletal strength decrease with age. But strength can be increased at any age through exercise.

STRENGTH

Can the design be upgraded further down the line? Do different parts of the design have different lifecycles?

UPGRADE

Flowmaker design creativity cards
(left and above)
Flowmaker is a design inspiration tool developed by the design group WEmake. All the cards can be freely accessed or purchased on the WEmake website, www.wemake.co.uk.

Part I
From design to
design thinking to
design activism

Chapter 2
Design thinking

2.3
Service design: maybe we don't need a product?

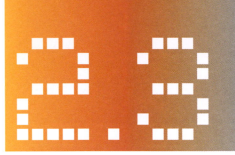

"Service designers visualize, formulate and choreograph solutions that are not yet available. They watch and interpret needs and behaviours and transform them into potential future services. In the process, exploring, generating and evaluating approaches are used similarly and a redesign of existing services is just as much a challenge as the development of new innovative services."

Birgit Mager
Professor for service design at
Köln International School of Design
www.designcouncil.org.uk

As we saw in Chapter 1 (see pages 22–23), service design focuses on the creation of integrated services, rather than isolated products. At the heart of service design is a consideration of the user experience. Designers are beginning to focus their attention much more on services rather than products, and 'service designer' is becoming increasingly common as a professional label. Yet services have clearly been around for a long time; so what does design bring to services that is new?

The design of pizza delivery

A user interacts with a service at a number of touchpoints. When we order a pizza delivery, we interact with the pizza delivery company in several ways: we select an order from a menu; we place the order via telephone or the Internet; we receive the delivery at our door and pay the delivery person.

There are many additional aspects of the service that we *don't* see. For example, how is our pizza prepared? How is it delivered? There are also aspects of the service that could be done in different ways; for example, at what point in the process do we pay for our order? When would be most convenient?

Every aspect of the service, including those we experience directly at the touchpoints and those we don't see, can be considered as a design outcome. In fact, a service can be seen collectively as a combination of a number of design outcomes, all of which interact successfully or unsuccessfully as the case may be. The design of a service, therefore, potentially involves a wide range of design specialisms. In our example, these would include graphic and communication design (a pizza menu); interaction design (the protocol used for placing an order and paying for it); product design (the pizza delivery box); even branding design (the corporate identity and reputation of the pizza company that means we even consider ordering from it in the first place).

A holistic perspective

Designers view the combination of individual elements that go to make up a service holistically. The ability to see all aspects and dimensions of a service at the same time, and be able to work towards the successful integration of all its separate elements, can be seen as the goal of service design. Service design is, therefore, based on *systems* thinking, and the successful integration of conventional design disciplines into a coherent, interacting whole.

Methodologically, service design is user-centred. A successful service brings the producer and consumer together effectively and efficiently; it succeeds because it delivers a good *experience* for both the user and the service provider. This is more likely to occur if the user is directly involved in the design and development of the service, through participatory design approaches. Services should be designed *with* users, not *for* them.

Service design: pizza delivery
(left)
A pizza delivery service is made up of a variety of different design outcomes, including graphic and communication design, product design and branding.

Part I
From design to
design thinking to
design activism

Chapter 2
Design thinking

Case study
Streetcar

**Streetcar, the London-based,
self-service, pay-as-you-go car club**
(below and below right)
Membership brings the convenience of
owning a car but without the costs and
hassle. Streetcars are parked in a dense
network of dedicated spaces across
London and several other UK cities,
making them easily accessible to users.
Once you pay to become a member,
you can start using any available
streetcar in four easy steps; book online
or by phone, swipe your card to open,
drive like it's your own and then return
when you're done.

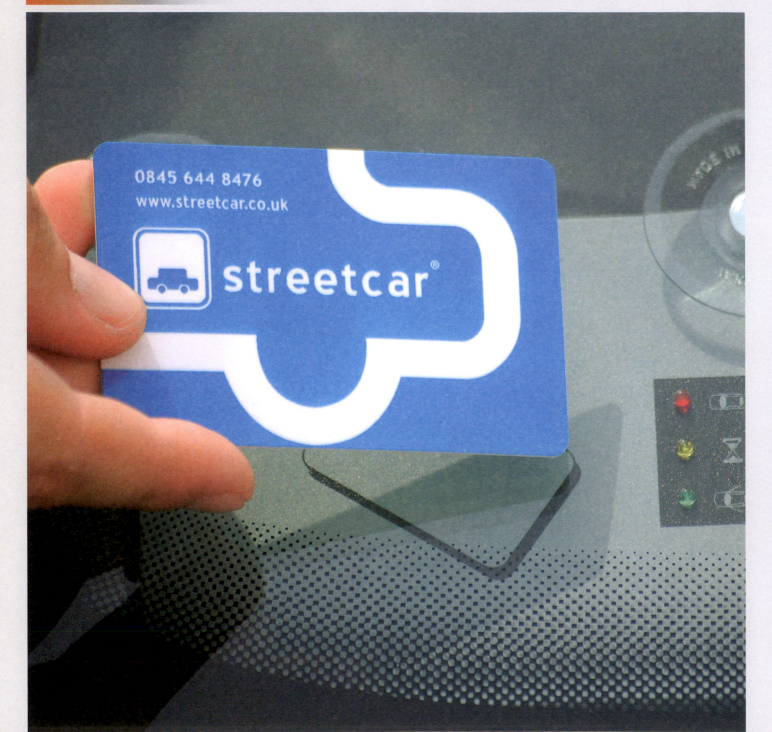

2.1   2.2   **2.3**   2.4   2.5   2.6
Service design: maybe we
don't need a product?

44 / 45

Streetcar is a self-service, pay-as-you-go car club, which has cars parked in a dense network of dedicated spaces across London and several other UK cities. The intention is that a prospective user of the service is within a few minutes' walk of a streetcar from their home or work.

How Streetcar works

Once you pay to become a member, a streetcar can be reserved online or by phone, and collected and returned at any time using a smartcard system. The vehicle fleet ranges from small cars to vans and seven-seaters. In contrast to the conventional car-rental period of 24 hours, a streetcar can be used for as little as 30 minutes. The cost of usage is based on how long you have the car and how far you drive. All other separate costs associated with owning a car (such as insurance, fuel and tax) are included in this single calculation. The company claims that, unless you're a heavy car-user, the annual cost of Streetcar will be dramatically less than owning a car, with lots of the hassle of car ownership removed.

What's new about Streetcar?

Car clubs are essentially a method of car sharing and so are nothing new. Neither is the idea of car rental. Where Streetcar has innovated is in the ease-of-use and flexibility of its service, from the local accessibility of its cars to the wide range of available rental periods. Streetcar also integrates its service with mobile consumer technologies, to allow users to change their rental arrangement in real-time from an internet-connected mobile phone (for example, simply texting the message 'extend 0.5' will increase your booking by an extra half an hour).

Few of the individual elements of Streetcar are unique. What is new is the integration of existing technologies into a service that is centred on delivering a convenient and satisfying user experience. Streetcar succeeds because it puts the user at the centre of effective and responsive service design.

live|work

live|work are the service design agency that collaborated with Streetcar to improve their offering. They contacted Streetcar because sustainability is a key issue they believe service design can address, and they try to apply the triple bottom line (see pages 92–93) to all their projects. This collaboration gave them the 'chance to apply their skills to a service that represented our values and our ultimate design challenge — shifting desirability from ownership to use.'

They shared an ambition with Streetcar to move the concept of car sharing into the mass market and, together with them, came to the conclusion that they had to elevate the experience of car sharing to a level where it would compete with the experience of car ownership: 'It was an obvious instance in which design could deliver economic, environmental, and social return on investment.'[3]

Book online or by phone   **Swipe** your card to open   **Drive** like it's your own   **Return** when you're done

[3] Løvlie et al (2008:76–77)

Part I
From design to
design thinking to
design activism

Chapter 2
Design thinking

2.4
Participatory design: from designing for to designing with

Participatory design attempts to actively involve all stakeholders (such as employees, customers, citizens and end-users) in the design process. The rationale is that this ensures that the final design solution meets actual needs and requirements and is usable by its intended audience. Participatory design is used in a variety of fields, including software, architecture and product design, to create design outcomes that are more responsive and appropriate to their users' practical, cultural and emotional needs. The logic is simple; if you are designing a solution to a problem, why not involve those who know the problem best and are the experts in relation to that problem? Why not involve the users?

How collaborative is participatory design?

Participatory design is an approach focused on processes and procedures of designing; it is not a design style. For some, this approach has a political dimension of user empowerment and design democratization. Participatory design practitioners share the view that every participant in a project is an expert in what they do, has valuable insights we can learn from and has a voice that needs to be heard. Spending time with users in their own environments, rather than working on a project abstractly in another space, is another important part of the participatory design process.

As specified in the design brief

As designed by the designer

As produced by the manufacturer

As installed at the user's site

What the user wanted

2.1   2.2   2.3   **2.4**   2.5   2.6
Participatory design:
from designing for
to designing with

46 / 47

A number of questions arise at this point. For example, how equal is the partnership between stakeholders and designers in the participatory design process? Can the stakeholders and the design professionals achieve an appropriate balance in their relationship? How are decisions made and final solutions reached? Is it an equal co-decision-making process?

A clear working framework needs to be in place. The ideal scenario is to agree on each stakeholder's particular contributions to the process and their influences on the developing design solution. The guiding principle is to share as much of the design thinking and decision-making power as possible.

The assumption is that the expertise does not reside solely with the design professionals but is also to be found in those whose interests are affected by the problem and its proposed solution. The participatory design process should not be based merely on *consultation* with an audience, but on their active participation. As John Thackara explains in the foreword to *Designers, Visionaries and Other Stories* (page xvii), 'Transformation on the scale we are now embarked on won't happen if we approach it top-down or outside in. If you find yourself designing emergency shelters for poor black people from the comfort of a Soho design studio, you are not up to speed on an important change: sustainable design means the co-design of daily life with the people who are living it.'

We're all designers now? The limits of co-creation

Broadening our idea of who designs to include not just designers but a range of other participants, raises a number of interesting questions. If all the members of a community are engaged in design thinking, do we still need a specialist designer? Can a campaign to improve the standard of children's school meals be considered an example of transformation, and so participatory design, even when there is ostensibly no design expertise, or designer, involved? What are the limitations of co-creation? Is the design that emerges from co-creation any good? How much creative autonomy and control of the design process should the designer surrender?

In *Sciences of the Artificial*, Herbert Simon famously declared that everyone designs who devises courses of action aimed at changing existing situations into preferred ones. We can agree with Simon, while remaining sceptical of the extent to which users can effectively design their own solutions. We still need design craft to convert the outcomes of design thinking into usable design outcomes. Designing with, rather than for, a community of users does not mean allowing them to design for themselves. The designer is still at the centre of the process, but working more inclusively.

Participatory design and design for sustainability

Participatory design has evolved independently of ecodesign, a design approach that considers the environmental impacts of the whole product life cycle. The two are brought together in design for sustainability, which adds an explicit emphasis on social responsibility to the environmental and ecological concerns of ecodesign. The participatory design approach fits with the Agenda 21 approach to achieving sustainable development, which emphasizes the importance of involving whole populations in broad processes to achieve large-scale change. The assumption is that without shared visions only short-term solutions are possible and these are unlikely to be the most sustainable solutions. Shared visions, reached through collaborative processes like participatory design, are most likely to deliver sustainable solutions of long-term value.

Participatory design
(left)
Participatory design attempts to actively involve all stakeholders (employees, customers, citizens, end-users) in the design process, with the aim of ensuring that the end solution meets actual needs and is usable by its intended audience.

Part I
From design to
design thinking to
design activism

Chapter 2
Design thinking

Case study
Engine design consultants

Founded in 2000, Engine is a leading service design and innovation consultancy based in London. Its team consists of designers, strategists, researchers and visualizers. Engine works with a wide range of private, public and third sector (non-profit and non-governmental) organizations.

Participatory design, or co-creation, is at the heart of what it does. Engine designs with users, in order to see beyond existing or proposed solutions, and help people discover their own responses to tackling a problem, or making the most of an opportunity. Engine's method is to guide discussions with users (using questions, provocations and tools) but also to allow users to participate and lead, as they are the real experts on themselves.

When this approach succeeds, the users of a prospective service gain a sense of ownership of the project and its outcomes, and may even become champions of the project and the process that brought it about. Projects conducted in this way are more enduring, as users gain the capacity to evolve the designed outcome in the future, having experienced why and how design decisions are made. This, coupled with appropriate tools, can help nurture a culture of innovation and change that remains when Engine's team has left.

"Co-design has challenged many professional designers because the idea of allowing anybody to have a go is seen as a threat to quality as well as a denial of skill and talent… A belief is that professional designers are valuable in new ways and not to the detriment of what designers have always done well. However the activity of designing responses to complex challenges is too important to leave only to designers."

www.enginegroup.co.uk

User participation
(above)
Users are the real experts on themselves and their situation, so are encouraged to take a leading role in exploring potential solutions and opportunities.

2.1   2.2   2.3   **2.4**   2.5   2.6
Participatory design:
from designing for
to designing with

48 / 49

Engine's co-creation process

Engine's co-creation process is built around three core phases, each with various stages built into them:

1 Identify

Orientation is about getting to know the organization Engine is working with. Workshops allow the project team to begin to share its views about the project context. In the Discover stage, Engine investigates how things are currently working from the perspective of those who use the organization's services, as well as those who provide them. These first two stages make up the Identify phase, and provide Engine with an understanding of the key issues and challenges to address and of what success might look like. It establishes what customers and providers value, in order to design services that deliver this value.

2 Build

In the Build phase, Engine conceptualizes and visually explores multiple responses to the challenge. This takes place at Engine's studios, in workshops that allow the clients, and often their customers, to roughly design their own services. Prototyping helps to reduce risk and get the best results, and this applies whether the design is for a service strategy or the touchpoints of a customer experience.

The next step is to model and test the generated ideas. Engine's staff are mainly designers, so this is a very visual and creative phase of the process. New propositions are brought to life in ways that allow them to be refined collaboratively with the client team and their customers.

3 Measure

Propositions are refined and evaluated iteratively. A point is reached at which the client and/or their customer, agrees they have arrived at what is needed. Being able to measure the efficiency and effectiveness — as well as the desirability, usefulness and usability — of a service is crucial for getting the feedback needed to support its ongoing improvement. This final phase, therefore, connects the end of the process with the beginning.

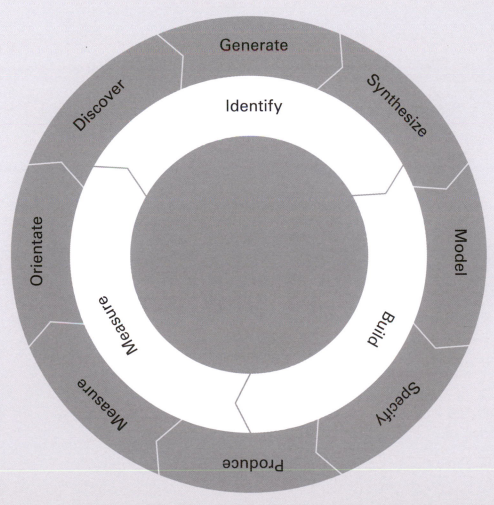

Participatory design process
(left)
Engine's co-creation process is divided into three key stages: identify, build and measure.

Part I
From design to
design thinking to
design activism

Chapter 2
Design thinking

2.5
Open source design

Design culture is becoming increasingly dominated by the figure of the celebrity designer. Leading designers are seen as the authors of the products they design. Products are increasingly branded by their designer, not just their manufacturer. Who designed a product is as important to the consumer as who manufactured it.

As a counter position to the celebrity designer, and to free up the potential impact of designs, the idea of open source has been created. It is a remix culture of designing, in which the originator of an idea passes it on to others who then take it in new directions, all of which dissolves clear authorship or attribution.

Creative Commons' logotypes
(above)
The Creative Commons licenses can be used by designers to indicate which rights they want to retain and which they are happy to give away in relation to their work. For example, the No Derivative Works license lets others copy, distribute, display, and perform only exact copies of your work. The Non-Commercial license lets others copy, distribute, display, and perform your work — and derivative works based upon it — but for non-commercial purposes only.

Creative Commons

The recent emergence of internet-based social networking has provided a platform for an explosion in open source designing and co-creating, a powerful tool for design activists. This has led to parallel innovations in intellectual property and copyright, such as the Creative Commons licensing system, through which authors of content (such as designers) can decide which rights to retain and which to give away in relation to their work.

Creative Commons is a non-profit corporation dedicated to making it easier for people to share and build on the work of others, consistent with the rules of copyright. It provides free licences and other legal tools to mark creative work with the freedom the creator wants it to carry, so others can share, remix, or use the work commercially. We'll look at some examples of this in Chapter 3 (see pages 58–61).

Foldschool
(above and left)
Nicola Enrico Stäubli offers his Foldschool furniture as a free download from www.foldschool.com. Just print it out, cut, and fold.

Part I
From design to
design thinking to
design activism

Chapter 2
Design thinking

Case study
Architecture for Humanity (AfH)

"We are building a more sustainable future through the power of professional design... Each year 10,000 people directly benefit from structures designed by Architecture for Humanity. Our advocacy, training and outreach programs impact an additional 50,000 people annually. We channel the resources of the global funding community to meaningful projects that make a difference locally."

Architecture for Humanity website
http://architectureforhumanity.org

Ambedker Nager Community Centre, India
(left)
Ambedkar Nagar is a village of Dalits (landless labourers). While it did not see heavy loss of life in the 2004 tsunami, it has victims of trauma and has suffered loss of livelihood from salt water flooding its farms. The tsunami was responsible for loss of crops that were due for harvesting. An AfH project built a community centre, to serve as a focal point of celebration and learning.

Architecture for Humanity (AfH) is an international non-profit organization promoting architectural and design solutions to social and humanitarian crises. Founded in 1999, AfH undertakes post-disaster reconstruction projects in places hit by sudden environmental catastrophe, such as Sri Lanka following the 2004 tsunami and New Orleans following Hurricane Katrina in 2005. AfH also uses architecture to respond to ongoing humanitarian issues, such as the lack of basic medical care in some parts of Africa. AfH believes that by encouraging architects to collaborate on these kinds of projects, they can generate solutions to social problems that might not otherwise be addressed.

AfH is a network of over 40,000 architectural professionals that serves a broad range of clients, including community groups, aid organizations, housing developers, government agencies and charitable foundations. In this way, many people can benefit from design, construction and development services who would not otherwise be able to afford them.

Locally appropriate solutions

AfH approaches social problems from an architectural perspective. Put simply, AfH asks what sort of improvements the design and execution of architecturally led projects could bring to local communities in need. Designing and building structures may not be the whole solution, but it can be a step in the right direction. It may be difficult to provide medical care without a clinic or hospital, for example. Equally, a conventional or converted hospital might not be as effective as a mobile clinic that can deliver health services directly to people in need. It is vital to assess local circumstances and needs.

AfH works through a series of national 'chapters'. This guards against the pitfalls of imposing universal or one-size-fits-all solutions on diverse and locally specific problems. For example, rather than building identical homes for people in need in Mexico, Florida, and Sudan, locally based AfH chapters will consider how people in each of those regions use their homes, what kind of local building materials are available and how the homes might be maintained by their occupants. Local AfH chapters have worked on rebuilding projects following natural disasters such as earthquakes, hurricanes and tsunamis. They have also provided housing for refugees and homeless people (see pages 160–161), playgrounds for children in war zones, and schools, sports facilities and job-training centres to enable people to help themselves. AfH project teams always partner with local groups or individuals.

Corporate partnerships

AfH also works with corporations to help implement, or establish, corporate social responsibility (CSR) projects. It has worked with Nike to set up a grants programme to fund the design and construction of safe places to play sport in communities that are typically overlooked. The scheme is aimed at locally based organizations and sees sport as a route to social improvement.

Projects can be anywhere in the world, but must have a commitment from an architect or building professional, or be willing to have one appointed to the project. For AfH, this is another route by which architectural expertise can be applied to social challenges, which many people might assume are not an obvious place for an architect to get involved.

Open architecture

AfH has also developed an online Open Architecture Network to allow architects, designers, builders – and their clients – to share architectural plans and drawings. Members can:

— Share their ideas, designs and plans.

— View and review designs posted by others.

— Collaborate with each other, people in other professions and community leaders to address specific design challenges.

— Manage design projects from concept to implementation.

— Communicate easily amongst team members.

— Protect their intellectual property rights using the Creative Commons 'some rights reserved' licensing system (see pages 50–51).

The creation of this online networking tool reflects AfH's belief that an inclusive and locally appropriate approach has a better chance of creating successful, and sustainable, architecture.

Part I
From design to
design thinking to
design activism

Chapter 2
Design thinking

2.6
There's nothing new about design thinking?

The emperor's new clothes
(above)
Is 'design thinking' anything new? Or is it just a new name for what design has always been about? Is use of the term a case of the emperor's new clothes?

"Design thinking is a public relations term for good, old-fashioned creative thinking."

Donald Norman
Design Thinking: A Useful Myth
www.core77.com

2.1   2.2   2.3   2.4   2.5   2.6
There's nothing new
about design thinking?

54 / 55

There are sceptical voices who question the recent emergence of design thinking as an apparently new discipline, and the reinterpretation of design that it seemingly entails. These sceptics ask: 'Haven't we always had design thinking, we just didn't call it that?' Design thinking is a new name, but is it really anything new?

As for the ambition of designers to be seen as saviours of society's biggest challenges, in the words of Jeremy Myerson, 'How far can you stretch design? What are the limits? How far can designers extend into other fields?'[4] Where does design end and politics begin? Should designers stick to designing what they know and were trained for? Are design, and designers, in danger of overreaching themselves? Is design thinking, with all its discussion of strategy, systems, just a new form of management consultancy? There are those who argue that, for example, transformation design is not really design because it doesn't look or feel much like design in the familiar sense of the word.

Design thinking and design craft

Design thinking is different from design craft. Design thinking is the ability to apply creativity to the formulation and resolution of problems and challenges. Design craft is the ability to translate this design thinking into design outcomes, either tangible (such as a product) or intangible (such as a service or behaviour). In advocating a broader application of design thinking, we should not undervalue the need for design craft. We should also remember that design craft is a valuable and hard-won capability, acquired through experience and training.

As the area currently called design thinking evolves, new more refined terminology is likely to continue to emerge. This may be confusing if lots of terms appear which seem to be trying to define almost the same thing. We should be careful not to dismiss the potential value of these new ways of thinking about design. But we should also maintain a healthy scepticism and be critical if we think they aren't really offering anything new.

Incremental change

In her article 'The revolution will not be designed' for *In These Times* (11 January 2008), Alix Rule claims that designers are in danger of overburdening themselves with the expectation that design thinking can tackle universal social goals such as eradicating poverty. She calls for realism rather than naive progressivism.

Rather than seeking to save the world in one fell swoop, designers should recognize the cumulative impact of incremental changes. While baby-steps and micro-innovations may not fulfil the lofty ambitions of the most vocal advocates of design thinking, they may nonetheless be effective in bringing about change in less spectacular ways. By using participatory, human-centered and integrated design approaches, designers are already playing a pivotal role in transforming individual and collective attitudes and behaviours.

"...those looking for a prescribed way to implement design thinking are destined to be disappointed. It's a messy, opaque process that depends as much on group dynamics as intellect or insight."

Helen Walters
Inside the Design Thinking Process
www.businessweek.com

[4] Myerson (2007)
www.designcouncil.org.uk

Part I
From design to
design thinking to
design activism

Chapter 3
Design activism

3.0

The emerging idea of design activism unites the active nature of design and designing with strong political awareness. This chapter explores the often radical ways in which design is now being used as a form of direct action, to transform society and the ways in which we live. The emergence of design activism raises some interesting questions. Can you be a design activist while working as a hired professional? How radical does design have to be in order to be considered activist?

This chapter also considers the related concept of design altruism and includes an interview with one of its leading exponents. There is also an interview with one of the foremost academic authorities on the emerging field of design activism, who argues that activism often strives for reform rather than transformation and can take place from anywhere within a system.

Part I
From design to
design thinking to
design activism

Chapter 3
Design activism

3.1
Design activism

"Design activism encompasses a wide range of real-life, socially and environmentally engaged actions. It includes processes that innovate forms of creative practice, providing models by which designers might work, or challenge existing conventions of design knowledge."

Leeds Festival of Design Activism, 2009
www.designactivism.org

Designers are generally apolitical (politically neutral) regarding their work, and don't see themselves as contributing to a grander narrative through what they do. Perhaps for this reason, few designers are motivated to become design activists. However, for those who do become involved, design activism unites the active nature of design and designing with strong political awareness.

The emerging notion of design activism attempts to account for the often radical ways in which design is being used to transform our society and the way we live, both now and for the future.

What is design activism?

Design activism is characterized both by its clear intent (the social or ecological cause being pursued) and the often radical nature of its practice (how design is used, and by whom).

Design activism is design that explicitly supports a particular cause, which is outside the core concerns of mainstream, commercially driven professional design practice. It has its roots in the mission-led design approaches that followed Victor Papanek's call to arms in his book *Design for the Real World*, such as Design for Development, Design for Need and, of course, Design for Sustainability.

Design activism is inherently radical because its goals, however they are defined in a specific instance, run counter to the dominant and sometimes all-enveloping commercial priorities of market-led professional design. Design activism is also self-consciously political, in that it often seeks to actively apply design practice and thinking for the benefit of under-represented or neglected sectors of society; for example immigrant communities or other social minorities. Design activists are often seeking to reconcile their personal beliefs with their professional practice as designers.

To be effective, design activism needs to have a purpose or intention, to be clearly targeted and to have a sense of the audience it is seeking to benefit. Otherwise we may end up with a mode of design activism that is self-indulgent, ill-informed, sanctimonious and grand-standing. Design activism should be concerned with bringing about positive social developments, not simply inciting anarchy. Terrorism can be seen as an extreme form of activism that is regressive (primarily against something and socially damaging) rather than progressive (in favour of something and socially constructive).

Design activism is also characterized by the nature of its practice. It is likely to be inclusive in seeking out alternative visions for society, so that it is not just designing for but also designing with the communities it seeks to help. Design activism must also be creative and imaginative in developing outcomes that contribute to delivering these new visions.

"[Design activism] is design thinking, imagination and practice applied knowingly or unknowingly to create a counter-narrative aimed at generating and balancing positive social, institutional, environmental and/or economic change."

Alastair Fuad-Luke
Design Activism: Beautiful Strangeness for a Sustainable World (2009:27)

Part I
From design to
design thinking to
design activism

Chapter 3
Design activism

Collaborative creation

Design activism is likely to be more effective when it is done in partnership with, for example, not-for-profit organizations who share the designer's aspirations to change the status quo. Pioneer design activists like Ennis Carter, founder and director of Design for Social Impact (see pages 70–71) have shown that to be effective in driving positive change, designers need to be well-informed and strategic. This comes from being a collaborative partner, rather than just a hired designer. This collaboration is more difficult and restrictive in certain design professions, such as industrial design, than in others.

The recent emergence of internet-based social networking has provided a platform for an explosion in open source designing and co-creating, a powerful tool for design activists.

Professional activism?

Design activism is, by definition, radical and challenging, and questions the way things are and how they are done. Yet most designers work within a professional framework most of the time. Design is, in most cases, a service for hire, and designers are usually employed by a client to work on a project that they did not initiate. This raises some interesting questions. How much scope is there for design activism within the professional designer's usual client-service relationship? Can design activism take place within an institutional context, or must it happen outside the obligations and constraints of a professional relationship?

This perhaps depends on the extent to which an organization or professional relationship allows the designer to challenge its principles and assumptions; for example, that financial profitability comes before any other consideration.

We might find it difficult to see how design that advocates change on behalf of a wronged, excluded or deprived group could easily emerge from a conventional professional design scenario. Does this mean the design activist should therefore be hostile to all organizations and institutions, including corporate design agencies? Not if we consider the designers who demonstrate that they can utilize design activism within commercial design consultancies such as Provokateur (see pages 30–31).

It may also be possible to work as a design activist within a larger agency with a strong ethical framework for their consulting, even if only on certain select accounts, such as those considered pro bono work, such as IDEO (see pages 158–159).

"I am interested in activism that advocates change on behalf of a wronged, excluded or deprived group – such as nature (or the climate), women in the workplace (such as women's wages), or victims of war, to name a few examples. Yet this kind of activism, a progressive advocating kind of activism, has largely seemed inappropriate or unworkable for designers. Why is this so?"

Ann Thorpe
Design – When is it Activism? (2008)
www.designactivism.net

How can designers engage in activism?
(above)
Plane Stupid, along with Greenpeace,
have campaigned against the planned
construction of a third runway at
London's Heathrow airport.

Part I
From design to
design thinking to
design activism

Chapter 3
Design activism

3.2
Activism through design

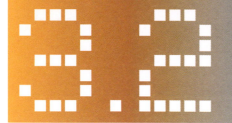

In considering design as an activist practice, we should also consider activism as a practice in its own right. This will allow us to consider examples of activism *through* design.

Who is an activist?

Who do we think of as an *activist*? The climate change campaigner? The anti-road protestor? The radical local politician? Many people in society work in some way to change the way things are, to raise awareness of a progressive cause, to right a societal wrong. Yet the activist goes further in pursuing these outcomes. Activism is militant and direct in its actions. In this, activism is distinct from agitation. Collecting signatures for a petition or wearing a red ribbon to raise awareness about AIDS can have an impact and bring about change, but they are clearly less direct than the examples shown throughout this chapter.

Those engaged in activism often deliberately and knowingly accept a degree of personal risk in doing so. For the activist, the cause he or she is fighting for can be more important than any personal or legal consequences; the end justifies the means.

Not all design is activist

We should consider the notion of design activism in this light. It now seems clear that all design is not *necessarily* activism, and that to think so is both to misunderstand the constraints within which much design operates, and also to undervalue the potential of activism for initiating radical change to the status quo. Commercially driven, client-led design is most suited to incremental change, as for example in automotive design's history of successive minor updates of stable product ranges. This is clearly not activist design in any meaningful sense.

Activism and the power of design

As well as considering design activism emerging from the design professions, we should also recognize that many leading practitioners of design activism are in fact non-designers. Visual communication design has long been used by political campaign groups. Many not-for-profit organizations value design and use the services of designers; for example large charities seeking to raise their profile and public donations often employ bold and well-designed publicity campaigns.

While designers are waking up to activism and looking for deeper values to direct their practice, activists are increasingly aware of the role design can play in furthering their own particular cause. While design is beginning to be radicalized, radicalism is also beginning to be better designed.

Your flight has an impact
(above and left)
Plane Stupid is a UK-based network of grass-roots groups that take direct, non-violent action against aviation expansion. Under the slogan 'your flight has an impact', Plane Stupid has used powerful, design-led visual imagery to show the potential consequences of unchecked aviation expansion.

Part I
From design to
design thinking to
design activism

Chapter 3
Design activism

Case study
Adbusters

"We are a global network of culture jammers and creatives working to change the way information flows, the way corporations wield power, and the way meaning is produced in our society."

www.adbusters.org

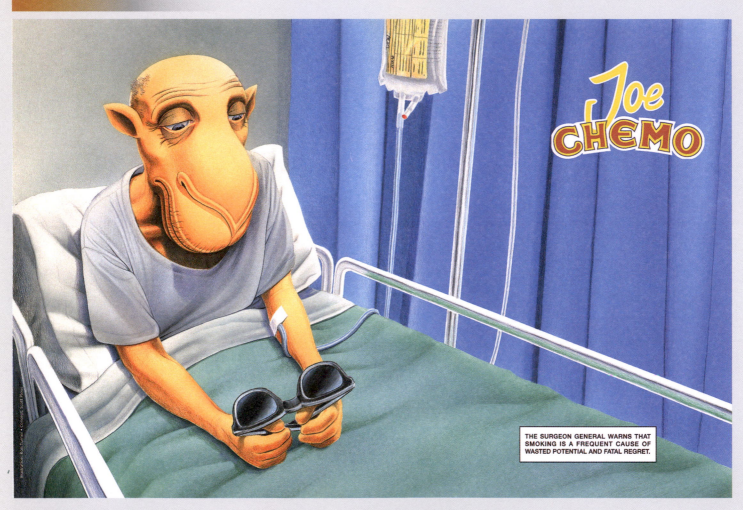

Culture jamming subverts the messages presented in advertising (above)
Adbusters is well-known for its advertising parodies. 'Joe Chemo' subverts cigarette advertising through professional-standard visual editing to illustrate the potential dangers of smoking.

Other parodies mock fashion and fragrance advertisements' promotion of unrealistic body image. A simpler and more direct approach is the 'skulling' of billboard advertisements. In a skulled advert, the model's face is crudely made to look like a skull to highlight the manipulative and damaging nature of the mass advertising system.

Perhaps the most visible design activists are the culture jammers. The most common form of culture jamming is the practice of parodying advertising in order to alter or subvert its messages. This kind of jamming is sometimes described using the analogy of the martial art of jujitsu; the power of a particular brand is exploited to undermine the explicit message of its advertisement, and draw attention to a hidden aspect of the company's story, for example alleged exploitative labour practices. In this way, particular commercial messages are subverted to become an 'uncommercial', in order to raise awareness of a deeper specific issue relating to the particular advert. However, this kind of practice is criticized for actually strengthening the grip of advertising and branding on our cultural space.

Although it may subvert the intended message, an uncommercial is still a commercial; it simply uses the power of advertising to direct us as passive consumers to a different end, for example to stop smoking rather than buy advertised cigarettes. Culture jamming campaigns have even been started by companies themselves who recognize the value they can add to their brand.

**Two-way communication
with advertisers**

A stronger version of culture jamming can be described as more thoroughly anti-capitalist, as it is concerned with challenging the status and methods of advertising itself rather than simply critiquing particular ads.

The primary motivation for this kind of intervention is resentment at the invasive and aggressive presence of commercial messages in public space. This mode of culture jamming strives to subvert the conventional one-way communication of advertising and open a dialogue between advertiser and consumer. It might involve hacking billboards, not to expose the particular brand featured but to highlight the manipulative nature of an ever-present advertising system that constantly encourages us to buy things we don't need and perhaps can't afford. This represents a move from pranksterism to politics, expressed via direct action in public space.

Adbusters: heroes or villains?

The best-known name in culture jamming is Adbusters. Adbusters Media Foundation is a not-for-profit, anti-consumerist organization founded in 1989 by Kalle Lasn and Bill Schmalz in Vancouver, Canada.

On the website www.adbusters.org, the foundation describes itself as, 'a global network of artists, activists, writers, pranksters, students, educators and entrepreneurs who want to advance the new social activist movement of the information age'.

Adbusters is well-known for its skilful and aesthetically perfect advertising parodies, but it does much more than this. It publishes a glossy magazine carrying its name, which cultivates culture jamming as an aesthetic form. It mounts campaigns such as 'Buy Nothing Day', through which we are encouraged to 'take a stand against the consumer culture that is killing our world'. It has even gone into business as a training shoe manufacturer; through its Blackspot shoe it intends to prove that running an ethical business is possible through an 'experiment with grass-roots capitalism'.

The range of its activities has made Adbusters controversial. Like all culture jammers, Adbusters seeks to challenge the examples and methods of advertising techniques, with financial consequences for targeted companies. Yet they have been accused of effectively commodifying consumption criticism; Adbusters has itself become a brand and an object of consumption, an advertisement for anti-advertising.

In this way, Adbusters are accused of playing the same game as the brands they target, and devaluing the politics of dissent that forms the basis of culture jamming. This view is supported by the fact that the methods of culture jamming have been appropriated by many of the very brands that were previously under attack. All radicalism is forgotten as corporate brands adopt the aesthetic of culture jamming to gently mock themselves and further strengthen their dominance.

The romantic image of the culture jammer is of the free-ranging activist, fighting the cultural dominance of the language of advertising. Yet the reality is that most producers of culture jamming, particularly as commodified in the magazine *Adbusters*, are likely to have day jobs in the advertising industry. Their success in the dominant commercially led communication system allows them to carry out their visual deconstructions of that same system by night. This form of culture jamming represents a mode of design activism that is complicit in the system it apparently seeks to subvert. Does it achieve anything, or is it self-indulgent and ultimately ineffectual?

Part I
From design to
design thinking to
design activism

Chapter 3
Design activism

3.3
Design altruism

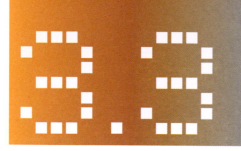

"For way too many people, 'changing the world' is equivalent to 'controlling the world', 'telling the world', 'educating the world'. I don't see many people understanding... that we can change the world by being changed by the world. It's always, my terms, our terms, our intentions, our actions, our ideas and in the end, it's just the same designer-as-hero bullshit to me, whether in Malawi, Kosovo, or Muncie."

Wes Janz
quoted in *Arguing with Success* by
David Stairs, 14 December 2009
design-altruism-project.org/?p=90

Many designers do not want to be 'handmaidens to the corporate bottom line'.[1] An alternative to commercially driven, client-led design practice is represented by the idea of altruism. The ideological and pragmatic failings of traditional for-profit design practice can be avoided through a form of non-competitive, mission-led design practice, driven by altruism.

Altruism is behaviour that benefits others at some cost to ourselves. This contrasts with selfishness, which is behaviour that benefits ourselves at some cost to others. Altruism is a social instinct, and reciprocal altruism (as opposed to selfish individualism) makes all communities stronger. Design altruism is, therefore, design practice and theory that is principally motivated by a commitment to benefitting the genuine needs of others, without the mediation and distortion of those needed by markets.

Design altruism is often discussed in relation to the twin agendas of design for need and design for development, particularly in relation to people in developing countries. There are examples of designers, design-led organizations and design academics who seek to dedicate their knowledge and skills wholly to altruistic projects, for example Motivation (see pages 156–157) and David Stairs (overleaf). However, this approach is difficult to maintain for most designers as it offers no guarantee of securing an income.

In his great polemic, *Design for the Real World*, Victor Papanek advocated the idea of a 'tithe', by which every designer should each year donate ten per cent of his or her ideas and talents to the service of the great majority of humankind that lack many of the basics of life. Many design companies now conduct pro bono work for cause-led clients, such as charities or social enterprises that would otherwise be unable to afford their professional design services.

While there is often promotional benefit for the design company in these cases, they do help to further the causes of clients who are not motivated by profit.

Whichever way a designer integrates altruistic work into their professional life, it can have a valuable influence on their sense of value and identity. Altruism allows designers to demonstrate that they can see beyond the confines of a commercially driven client relationship. It does designers good to apply their professional capabilities to a cause that they are committed to and think worthwhile, irrespective of whether or not there is financial gain in pursuing it.

Participatory design
(left)
These images show Albert John Mallari (MA Design for Development, Kingston University, London) working with Eduk Inc., a social enterprise based in the Philippines. The work involves designing community learning resource centres in poverty-stricken areas using participatory design approaches. Albert believes design-based interventions can significantly raise the level and nature of impact development activities can have on client communities.

[1] Stairs (2005:6)

Part I
From design to
design thinking to
design activism

Chapter 3
Design activism

Interview
David Stairs

WILL WORK FOR SEROTONIN

David Stairs
Executive Director of
Designers Without Borders

What is Designers Without Borders?

Designers without Borders (DWB) is a consortium of designers and design educators, working to assist institutions of the developing world with their communication needs. Its volunteers provide instruction, consultation and development advice and assistance in both community and educational environments. In other words, we deliver technology, instruction and design consulting to schools and select non-profits.

DWB was founded in Kampala, Uganda, when my family and I were there on a two-year Fulbright residency in 2001. It was incorporated as a non-profit the following year. Why Africa? I was a child in the 1960s, and the Nigerian civil war of Biafra had a profound effect on me.

When I returned to the US after those two years, it seemed to me that the design world was on the verge of embracing socially relevant design. There was a mild ripple of interest, mostly from younger designers ostensibly looking for alternative design practice opportunities.

What is design altruism?

'Is altruism a methodology or a principle?' is a perennially popular question. The answer is: both. Methodology suggests agency, a more feet-on-the-ground, applied approach than just a set of ethics or concepts. People have asked me, 'What the hell does "design-altruism" mean anyway? Do you really think altruism is the solution for social problems?' And I'll answer, 'Of course I do', which gets me into many long-winded debates. Is altruism the same as pro bono? I think altruism is to pro bono as the human gene pool is to a newborn infant.

What are the limits of design altruism?

One would like to believe that there are no such limits, but they are being tested every day. Although they would likely disagree, Architecture for Humanity, an organization I've promoted for years, has evolved into little more than an emergency relief agency. This is an effective fund-raising strategy because busy people open their purses for disaster scenarios. Others have discovered altruism's marketability and are rushing to fill the void. When altruism becomes commercialized, by firms such as IDEO and others, we've reached its effective limits. Commercial design is market-led.

Effective altruistic design leads, it's not led. It's preventative, not knee-jerk, reactive or determined by any avaricious inclination.

Is there a project that demonstrates your idea of design altruism?

I'd have to say a good model is Greg Mortenson's Central Asia Institute, whose mission is 'Peace and Hope Begin With Education: One Child At A Time'. This is not a design initiative at all, but an excellent example of an in-person capacity-building initiative that focuses on what matters: education, girls and women, health care in rural areas, conflict prevention and development. It's what I wish DWB to be, and how we proceed with it. Unlike other projects that might share the same rhetoric, Central Asia Institute isn't just a band-aid for the well-meaning, nor a poster child for top-down design intervention from the developed north.

The Design Altruism Project is an attempt to create an interactive online community for the purpose of discussing altruism from the perspective of design. We try to present a wide range of ideas, stories and opinions from the novice to the highly experienced.

Central Asia Institute is a non-profit organization founded in 1996
(left)
It runs community projects in remote, under-served mountain communities in northern Pakistan, Afghanistan, Kyrgyzstan and the steppes of Mongolia. It promotes self-sustainability through a commitment to local project leadership and has a policy of non-affiliation to any particular group.

Each one of the Institute's projects is locally initiated and involves community participation. A committee of elders guides each selected project. Before a project starts, the community matches project funds with equal amounts of local resources and labour. This commitment ensures a project's viability and long-term success.

Part I
From design to
design thinking to
design activism

Chapter 3
Design activism

Case study
Design for
Social Impact

Since the 1960s, designers have struggled to define their larger role in the world. Students enter design school with youthful optimism and often come out at the end of their course ready to change the world. Unfortunately, in most professional practices that enthusiasm meets a sobering truth that design serves commerce and commercialism. While nearly every firm does its share of pro bono work, the needs of paying clients almost always come first. That's why it's so refreshing to come across designers who have managed to put their social conscience ahead of the bottom line. Ennis Carter, founder and director of Design for Social Impact, is one such example.

The mission

Ennis Carter never set out to be a designer. After getting her philosophy degree from New York University, she went to work for the New Jersey Public Interest Research Groups (PIRGs). It was there, in the low-budget (and sometimes no-budget) non-profit world, that she discovered a love and affinity for design. While working as a young organizer for PIRGs in the late 1980s, Carter found herself, out of necessity, making her own posters for events and rallies. Along the way, she became captivated by the power of graphic design to communicate social messages, and gradually shifted the focus of her work in that direction. In 1996 she founded Design for Social Impact (DfSI).

Design for Social Impact is a low-cost visual communications agency that combines 'artistry and activism' to call attention to important social issues:

— '**Artistry** a high-level skill that you can learn by study and practice and observation.

— **Activism** an engaged practice of living where actions reflect core values and the results are beneficial.'

Buy Fresh Buy Local campaign
(left)
A US national identity campaign to encourage shoppers to visit local farmers' markets and buy locally grown, produced and sold foods. To assure consistency across the US and internationally, Design for Social Impact worked with FoodRoutes Network on message development, public awareness campaign design and ongoing identity brand management. The campaign is in around 30 US states and counting.

DfSI works with organizations and community groups who are promoting issues and actions that are in the public interest. It also helps groups to communicate their vision through effective use of visual communication design, using:

— Organizational identity evaluation

— Audience mapping

— Strategic message design

— Visual identity and campaign design

— Writing and editing

— Website strategy design and programming

The risky venture caught on and Ennis Carter's graphics started giving cash-strapped organizations a fighting chance to compete for attention against the slickest corporate advertising. Her secret weapon has been leveraging her own knowledge of the non-profit world to mount successful campaigns without the benefit of expensive market research or focus groups. She also runs her firm at cost, which allows the company to offer professional design services at roughly half the price of a traditional firm. Fees are based on the overall cost of running the operation, without building in a profit margin. There's also a concerted effort to keep overheads low.

The value of good design

With limited resources, DfSI's campaigns hinge on the power of graphic design to motivate large groups of people. Many of the company's clients can't afford a typical design firm, so staying within budget is always a priority. For example, they developed a simple message 'Save Our Roots' for a campaign to prevent the construction of new chip mills in Missouri (notorious for clear-cutting forests) until a sustainable forest protection plan could be developed. This common-sense phrase drove the overall look of the printed materials, which convey a sense of common heritage.

Working on design projects with non-profit organizations has its own set of challenges. Miniscule client budgets mean no high-end photography shoots or production techniques. These are challenges that the DfSI team is constantly faced with, and which they have to consistently overcome. More importantly, non-profit organizations using design to communicate their message are also often hampered by their lack of understanding of the value of good design.

While this can also be true of other clients, it takes on a whole new meaning in the non-profit sector. Ennis says that in the minds of some non-profits, good design can come across as indulgent, which is not the impression most cash-strapped organizations want to make.

The DfSI team, therefore, has to work hard to convince their clients that good design doesn't have to look slick, and that they can create designs that are accessible and entirely appropriate. Working with non-profits often requires compromises and designers who are extremely committed to their design activism. As a key DfSI tenet states: 'Improving lives is more important than selling products.'

Today, Design for Social Impact has a staff of eight and a volunteer internship programme that adds another five to ten people to the office at any one time. The firm's client roster includes organizations from The Domestic Violence Project and Meatless Monday, to the Clean Air Council and World Wildlife Fund. 'I think people have to be moved personally by issues or other people's stories before they get involved', says Carter. 'We inspire people through affirmation, beauty and hope.'

Part I
From design to
design thinking to
design activism

Chapter 3
Design activism

Interview
Ann Thorpe

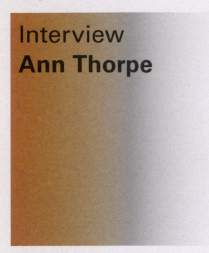

Ann Thorpe
Author of *The Designer's Atlas of Sustainability*

How did you get into the area of design activism?

After much work on sustainable design, what bothered me was the tension between the business case for sustainable design and design's broader (non-business) contributions to sustainability, which feel more like social activism. But the business case gets far more attention; it's taken as more legitimate. Also sustainable design, useful as it is in some ways, has grown into a concept that is almost too big and general for developing designers' roles. So it seems helpful to be more explicit about the activist role and specific causes. I wondered how activism is studied elsewhere, and that led me to my current work.

Can design activism take place within an institutional context, or must it happen outside the obligations and constraints of a professional relationship?

In my view, design activism can occur from anywhere within the economy. And by economy, I mean the larger system that includes the private sector (businesses), the public sector (government) and the non-profit sector (charities and advocacy groups). In fact my research shows that design activism is often instigated by public agencies and in more cases than you might think, by businesses. For example, cities often strive to demonstrate design for change in the development of new schools, public libraries, courthouses, or elements of the urban fabric such as street furniture or parks.

A recent spate of new public libraries in the United States — for example in Seattle, Salt Lake City, and Los Angeles — has shown cities soliciting quite activist buildings that challenge conceptions about public space, access and knowledge.

I think a key issue here is that a great deal of activism strives for change in terms of reform rather than transformation. Many well-known, historical activist struggles were also reformist in nature.

Whitechapel Idea Store, London
(right)
The Whitechapel Idea Store seeks to be more than a repository of books and computers. The image opposite shows a Silver Surfer lesson, teaching senior citizens how to get the most out of the Internet. The design of the building attempts to redefine the role of a library and broaden the ways in which it can serve its community. Is this design activism?

The struggle for women, or for black people, to get the vote did not involve attempting to change the one-person-one-vote system. Instead, these struggles sought to reform the system so that more people could participate in it. While some of the tactics these campaigners used were radical, even militant, other tactics (such as collecting petition signatures) were not. Similarly, much of design activism calls for better versions of existing systems, rather than entirely new systems. For example, we're not going to do away with schools, but we do want significant reform in many of the physically designed aspects of schools; from the walls to the textbooks.

Reformers fit more comfortably within institutional settings because reform is less daunting than transformation – where transforming the education system might involve doing away with schools as we know them. In terms of tactics, activism is also dynamic. What seemed radical in the past, such as the tactic of protest marches, is perceived as more moderate today.

Ultimately, design activism is a collective performance with a lot of players on stage – clients, designers, users, the media, regulators, suppliers and so forth. Typically some players are within institutions, even if others come from outside. People move among institutions over the course of careers and in a networked society it is sometimes hard to find an outside. So it is difficult to say that there is one right place for design activism or a correct style of tactic.

What do you see as the significant differences between the terms 'design activism' and 'design altruism'?

I see design altruism as a subset of design activism. Although the definition of altruism is a somewhat general notion of unselfishness, I think it often implies work without compensation, or poorly paid volunteer work. And a lot of emergency relief activity, for example, would fall into this category. By contrast, design activism covers a spectrum; from volunteer work to well-paid employment.

Granted these are different flavours of activism, but arguably they all use design artefacts and processes to reveal better visions for society and to actively disrupt the status quo.

In my research, I saw design altruism emerging in a variety of cases, such as when 600 architects volunteered with the American Institute of Architects to help in recovery efforts after Hurricane Katrina, or when an architecture firm got involved with a disadvantaged elementary school because the school was located across from the firm's office.

Part II
Sustainability

Part II examines the often hugely problematic contemporary notion of sustainability. The 'S' word can often mystify more than illuminate our thoughts on where we want our society to go. Indeed, the term sustainability is often used interchangeably with sustainable development. Confusion as to what sustainability is can hamper our attempts to respond to it as an agenda, in design as much as in any other activity, sector or discipline.

Chapter 4
The 'S' word

4.0

A number of models of sustainability are presented in this chapter, all of which emphasize that sustainability has both an environmental and a humanitarian agenda. Poverty alleviation and environmental protection are intrinsically linked, and one cannot be meaningfully addressed while the other is ignored. This chapter also examines ways of measuring sustainability and asks how useful these might be.

Sustainability is an apparently simple concept, made up of a complex array of sometimes competing considerations. It requires a holistic view of the world and our place within it. The term sustainability is asked to do a huge amount of work and we should be careful how we use it. The chapter closes with an interview with an internationally renowned environmentalist who considers the language of sustainability.

4.1
What do we want to sustain?

4.2

The term sustainability means an ability to sustain, to endure over time. For example, a company with a sustainable business plan is looking forward to surviving for perhaps the next five years. But the term is now widely used in a more particular sense to mean ecological longevity. In other words, will we as a species be around in a hundred years time, or will we have too seriously harmed the earth's capacity to support us?

Sustainable development?

The modern sustainability agenda is usually presented in terms of the concept of sustainable development. Our dominant contemporary idea of sustainability derives from the so-called Brundtland definition of 'development that meets the needs of the present without compromising the ability of future generations to meet their own needs'.[1] This assumes that there can be such a thing as sustainable development, that we can maintain economic growth and our affluent modern lifestyles while preserving the earth and its natural systems.

John Constable, 'The Hay Wain' (1821)
(right)
An idealized depiction of a past that never was?

Some commentators are sceptical of this assumption. For them, human industrial development is the cause of our present and growing ecological problems, and sustainable development is simply not a viable prospect. James Lovelock, originator and champion of Gaia theory, goes so far as to say that it is too late for sustainable development; we cannot now avert the damaging global ecological consequences of industrialization and so should think in terms of a sustainable retreat from its worst effects.

We are part of nature

Sustainable development, as it is usually defined, is also an inherently anthropocentric (human-centred) concept. By assuming human dominion over the natural world, this idea of sustainable development fails to clearly acknowledge our absolute dependence on the earth's supporting systems for our survival. Ann Thorpe's refined definition acknowledges this dependence more clearly: 'development that cultivates environmental and social conditions that will support human well-being indefinitely'.[2]

Gaia theory teaches us that we as humans are a part of, not separate from, the biological functions of the planet that sustains us. It is therefore dangerous to assume that we can manage the earth and its systems as if we were not intrinsically bound-up in its ecology. It is misguided to talk about the environment, as if we are somehow separate from it. There is not nature and then us; we are part of nature. It is our failure to recognize this that has contributed to the ecological threats, such as predicted climate change, that we now face.

When we talk of saving the planet, what we really mean is preserving the earth's capacity to support human life. The planet will certainly outlast us no matter what ecological havoc we wreak. Sustainability, to be a meaningful and useful concept, must therefore embrace the idea of a global ecology, and its meaning must be expanded to include all parts of nature (not just humanity) and allow all of nature to meet its own needs, now and in the future. The earth's biosphere in its current liveable state is a balanced, self-adjusting system. When we dramatically alter that balance, for example through deforestation of Borneo or the Amazon, we harm our own prospects of survival as well as those of other species.

The idea of progress

We should also resist any urge to return to a romanticized pre-industrial past in which human ecological impacts were much less great than they are today. Instead, we can usefully ask the question, what do we want to sustain? For example, John Constable painted 'The Hay Wain' in 1821, depicting a scene at Flatford Mill on the River Stour in the southern English county of Suffolk. If we return to the same spot now the scene will look quite different to its representation in the painting. Yet, if we were there in Constable's time, the scene would still not be exactly as depicted in his painting.

Equally, we should be careful of embracing the promise of technological progress too enthusiastically. We are perhaps wise to exercise the precautionary principle: if an action or policy has suspected social or environmental risks, we should be cautious in pursuing it until it is proven to be safe, as for example in the case of nuclear power generation.

We should look to the future while learning from the past. A commitment to human 'progress' can be dangerous if we forget to learn from our past mistakes. But this does not mean that we should reject the idea of progress out of hand and idealize a lost way of living that never existed in the way we might imagine it.

[1] World Commission on Environment and Development (1987). (Also known as The Brundtland Report.)

[2] Thorpe (2007:7)

4.2
Models of
sustainability

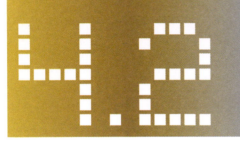

Issues of poverty and environmental change are intrinsically linked
(right and below)
Developing countries are the first to experience the harmful effects of climate change. Poverty is likely to be a consequence of problems such as water scarcity, crop failure and increased risk of flooding.

People in developing countries aren't thinking about how climate change will affect them.

They already know.

Right now in some of the world's poorest countries, droughts and floods are more frequent and intense as a direct result of changing weather patterns. Every day, Oxfam is working with families to protect their homes and harvests. You too can help tackle the human impact of climate change.

 Text "HERE" to 87099 to get involved.

Climate change costs lives. Let's sort it Here & Now.

Be Humankind 🎗 **Oxfam**

SMS texts charged at your standard network rates. Oxfam is a registered charity in England and Wales No 202918 and Scotland SC 039042. Oxfam GB is a member of Oxfam International

Some people are finding climate change particularly hard to stomach.
And with their children going hungry, who can blame them?

Right now in the developing world, extreme weather conditions mean the only thing farmers are growing is hungry. Every day, Oxfam is working with them to build flood defences and plant drought resistant seeds. You too can help tackle the human impact of climate change.

Here & Now Text "GROW" to 87099 to get involved.

Climate change costs lives. Let's sort it Here & Now.

Be Humankind 🎗 **Oxfam**

Sustainable development is a diverse concept; it is an umbrella term covering a broad range of views. Therefore its scope or content is not confined to what are generally perceived as environmental issues, such as climate change, although different advocates do give different emphases to different issues.

UNESCO's ten key themes

The United Nations Educational, Scientific and Cultural Organization's (UNESCO) decade of Education for Sustainable Development (ESD) suggests ten key themes (listed below).

These key themes are interrelated and may be explored in a variety of contexts and at a range of scales, such as nationally or locally. These issues come from three spheres: environment, society and economy. Environmental issues, such as water and waste, affect every nation – as do social issues such as employment, human rights, gender equality, peace and human security.

Every country also has to address economic issues, such as poverty reduction, corporate responsibility and accountability. Major issues that have grabbed global attention — such as HIV/AIDS, migration, climate change and urbanization — involve more than one sphere of sustainability. As experts point out, such issues are highly complex and the citizens and leaders of this and the next generation must develop sophisticated strategies to find solutions.

How do we take this sustainable development theory and build a plan of possible practices that serve to assist citizens, communities, or organizations and businesses to move towards behaving sustainably? Numerous academics, governments, consultants and organizations have developed sustainability models for investigation and imitation that address how sustainable development can be better understood and applied from various perspectives and levels.

Poverty alleviation or environmental protection?

People in developing nations may feel that their primary concern is poverty alleviation and that environmental protection is a secondary consideration. Yet poverty and environmental degradation are inextricably linked. Addressing poverty without also considering the ecological impacts of our actions may provide short-term relief, but is likely to make things worse in the long term. For example, rainforest deforestation provides lucrative short-term financial rewards, but it is damaging to prospects of human survival in the long term.

Poverty alleviation only makes sense when framed by an awareness of environmental consequences. Single-minded economic development is not the best long-term route out of poverty if it simply creates more problems for the future. Put simply, we cannot thrive when our environment is unable to support us.

"…widespread poverty is no longer inevitable. Poverty is not only an evil in itself, but sustainable development requires meeting the basic needs of all and extending to all the opportunity to fulfil their aspirations for a better life. A world in which poverty is endemic will always be prone to ecological and other catastrophes."

World Commission on Environment and Development 1987: **Overview** (paragraph 27)

UNESCO's ten key themes	
1	Overcoming poverty
2	Gender equality
3	Health promotion
4	Environmental protection and conservation
5	Rural transformation
6	Human rights
7	Intercultural understanding and peace
8	Sustainable production and consumption
9	Cultural diversity
10	Information and communication technologies

Three pillars of sustainable development

The popularity of sustainability stems also from a simple model used to facilitate the comprehension of the term and the relations of the three following dimensions:

— People (social)

— Planet (environment)

— Profit (economic)

The United Nations 2005 World Summit Outcome document refers to the 'interdependent and mutually reinforcing pillars'[3] of sustainable development as economic development, social development and environmental protection.

.

Three concentric circles model

For many environmentalists, the idea of sustainable development is an oxymoron as development always seems to entail environmental degradation. From this perspective, the economy is a subsystem of human society, which is itself a subsystem of the biosphere, and a gain in one sector is a loss from another. This can be illustrated as three concentric circles (see opposite).

As the concentric circles diagram illustrates, the economy exists entirely within society, because all parts of the human economy require interaction among people. However, society is much more than just the economy. Friends and families, music and art, religion and ethics are important elements of society, but are not primarily based on exchanging goods and services. Society, in turn, exists entirely within the 'environment'. Our basic requirements (air, food and water) come from the biosphere, as do the energy and raw materials for housing, transportation and the products we depend on.

The concentric circles model reminds us that the biosphere surrounds society and that society can never be larger than what it can support. At earlier points in human history, the environment largely determined the shape of society. Today the opposite is true: human activity is reshaping the environment at an ever-increasing rate.

This sustainable development model acknowledges that there are limits to the natural, social and built systems upon which we depend. The economy is dependent on the health of society, which in turn is dependent on the health of the biosphere.

The three pillars model of sustainable development
(right)
The three pillars model emphasizes the equal importance of each pillar. If any one aspect is ignored, or given a higher priority than the others, the effect will be to unbalance and destabilize all three aspects, because they are inter-connected and interdependent. It is also recognized that these three aspects need to be addressed simultaneously – we cannot address them one at a time as this would also create an imbalance.

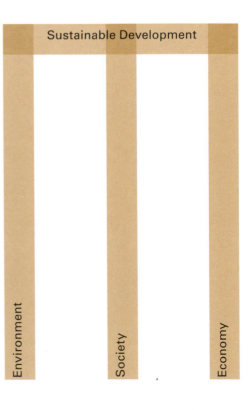

Sustainable Development

Environment

Society

Economy

[3] United Nations General Assembly (2005:12).

[4] UNESCO (2001: Preface and Article 3).

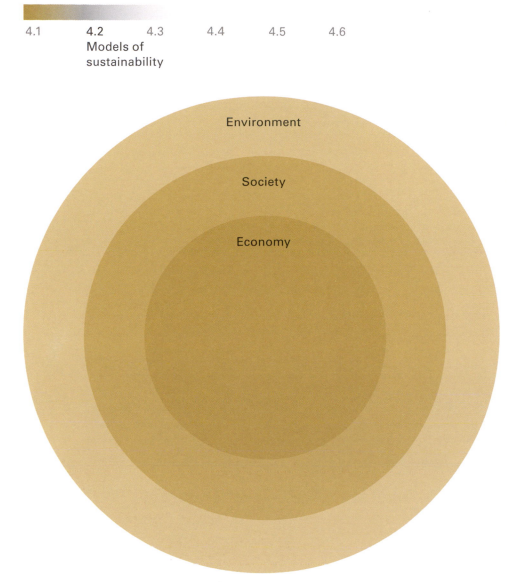

**Concentric circles model of
sustainable development**
(left)
The economy exists within society, and
both the economy and society exist
within the environment.

**The overlapping circles model of
sustainable development**
(right)
We need to continue to evolve an
understanding of the value system
encapsulated in the three pillars
definition of sustainable development.
Various representatives of indigenous
peoples have argued that there
is a fourth pillar of sustainable
development – cultural diversity. As
stated by UNESCO's Director-General
Koïchiro Matsuura: '…cultural diversity
is as necessary for humankind as
biodiversity is for nature'; it becomes
'one of the roots of development
understood not simply in terms
of economic growth, but also as a
means to achieve a more satisfactory
intellectual, emotional, moral and
spiritual existence'.[4]

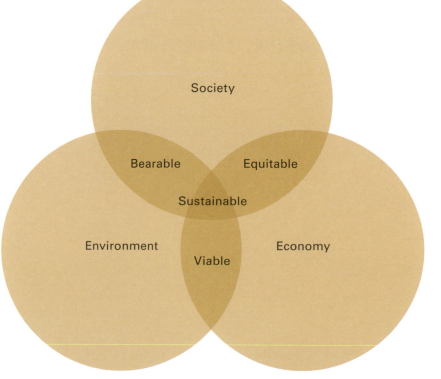

4.3
Measuring sustainability

**United Nations Human Development
Index map of the world 2007**
(right)
The United Nations Human
Development Index is used to rank
countries globally by their level of
human development, incorporating
a wide range of economic, social and
ecological factors. The key dimensions
are a nation's citizens' life expectancy,
knowledge and education (often
focusing on literacy) and standard
of living.

hdr.undp.org/en/statistics

High Human Development

Medium Human Development

Low Human Development

Not Ranked

4.3
Measuring
sustainability

Indicators of sustainable development review progress; they highlight where the challenges are and they help us to understand what sustainable development means globally, nationally, locally and personally as individuals. Attempts are made to measure sustainable development using sets of numerical indicators. These sets of sustainability indicators are often combined to produce an index or overall score. An index will focus on a particular scale: global, local or individual.

The commonly accepted Brundtland definition of sustainable development discusses meeting the needs of the present without compromising the ability of future generations to meet their own needs. Sustainable development indicators, such as those shown by the UK's Department for Environment, Food and Rural affairs (available at www.defra.gov.uk), show us that, globally, we are not even meeting the needs of the present.

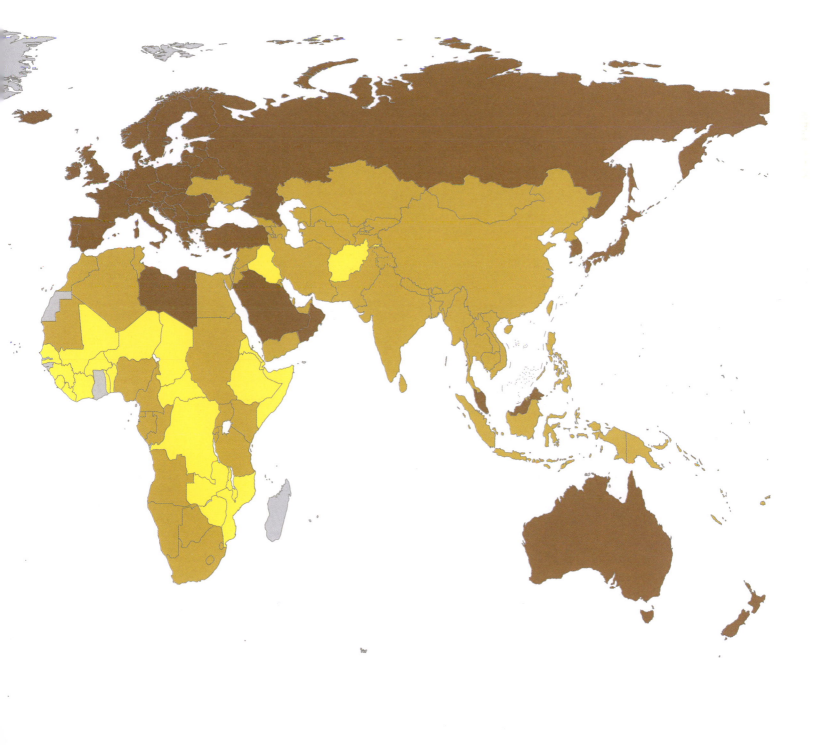

Numbers aren't everything?

How successful can sets of numerical indicators be in assessing or representing sustainable development? Indicators are confined to what can be measured numerically. Indexes can be made up of quite complex sets of indicators, but will always be a simplification of the full picture. There will inevitably be aspects of sustainability that the indicators fail to capture. We should therefore be wary of accepting indicators as a perfect proxy for sustainable development in a particular case.

Eco footprinting

The ecological footprint is a measure of human demand on nature. It measures the area of land and water a human population requires to produce the resources it consumes and to absorb its waste using existing technology. Using this assessment, it is possible to estimate how much of the earth (or how many planet earths) it would take to support humanity if everybody lived a given lifestyle.

We can measure the footprint of a population on varying scales – as an individual or business, city or even a nation. The aim is for us to be able to manage our ecological assets more wisely and take personal and collective action to live within the earth's bounds. While the term ecological footprint is widely used, methods of measurement vary. However, calculation standards are now emerging to make results more comparable and consistent.

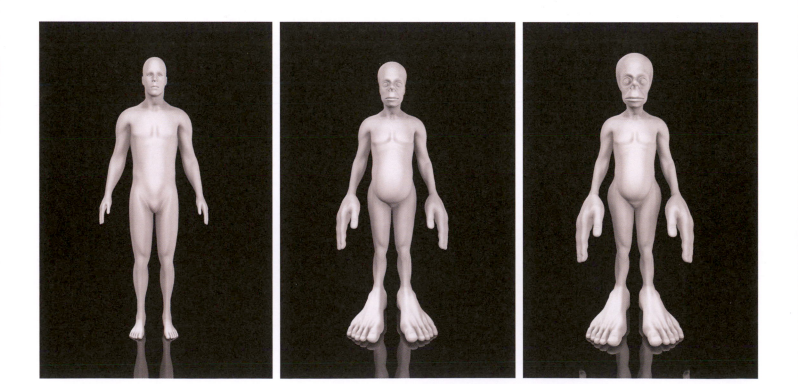

**Costa Rica came top of the
Happy Planet Index in 2009**
(right)
The Happy Planet Index (HPI) doesn't
reveal the 'happiest' country in the
world. It shows the relative efficiency
with which nations convert the planet's
natural resources into long and happy
lives for their citizens. The HPI shows
high levels of resource consumption
do not reliably produce high levels of
well-being. The index is produced by
the New Economics Foundation, an
independent 'think-and-do tank' that
engages in economics as if people and
the planet mattered.

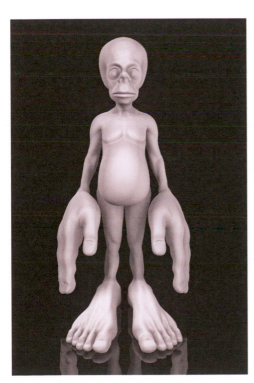

**RSA Changing Habbits:
Personal ecological footprinting**
(left)
The Habbits are humanoid forms with
body parts distorted relative to the
environmental impact of common
activities. The body parts grow larger
where an individual's impact is higher.
Each body part is assigned to one
impact:
Head = Electrical goods
Mouth = Water
Hands = Home energy
Stomach = Food
Bottom = Waste
Feet = Transport

Case study
BioRegional's
One Planet Living

Sustainable development, with its global agendas and issues, can seem complex, confusing and overwhelming from an individual standpoint. One can question; how can I start to make sense of this arena? What can I do as an individual to address these issues?'

BioRegional is trying to address these questions with their 'One Planet Living' practical projects and partnerships, which aim to demonstrate how we can all live within our fair share of the earth's resources.

Pooran Desai and Sue Riddlestone co-founded BioRegional in 1992, in the UK. Their aim was to address over-consumption of resources, which they believe is the major driving force for environmental degradation. The organization is a charity but it is also entrepreneurial and has begun a number of enterprises. They have always intended BioRegional's projects to be models that can be taken into the mainstream economy, either through the establishment of new companies or by working in partnership with existing companies as is evident in the BedZED project (see pages 126–127).

BioRegional's One Planet logotype
(left)
One Planet aims to inspire sustainability around the world. The logo is used by community, government and business partners to denote that they are part of the initiative. These partners must reach tough standards and environmental charity BioRegional audits their progress annually.

BioRegional's approach
Measuring — Solving — Delivering — Inspiring

Measure impacts

Uses scientific techniques to quantify environmental impacts and identify opportunities to make significant reductions across all areas of their ecological footprint.

Devise solutions

Uses tools such as the ten principles to devise solutions and plan the actions they need to take to achieve One Planet Living.

Deliver sustainability

Sets up partnerships and new enterprises to effectively deliver their practical sustainability solutions.

Inspire others

Aims to inspire and assist others to adopt their solutions by providing a range of services and communicating the lessons of their practical projects.

BioRegional's ten principles of One Planet Living

The ten principles of One Planet Living are used as a framework for their various programmes.

1 Zero carbon
Making buildings more energy efficient and delivering all energy with renewable technologies.

2 Zero waste
Reducing waste, reusing where possible, and ultimately sending zero waste to landfill.

3 Sustainable transport
Encouraging low-carbon modes of transport to reduce emissions. Reducing the need to travel.

4 Sustainable materials
Using sustainable products that have a low-embodied energy.

5 Local and sustainable food
Choosing low-impact, local, seasonal and organic foods and reducing edible and packaging waste.

6 Sustainable water
Using water more efficiently in buildings and in the products we buy; tackling local flooding and watercourse pollution.

7 Natural habitats and wildlife
Protecting and expanding old habitats and creating new space for wildlife.

8 Culture and heritage
Reviving local identity and wisdom; support for and participation in the arts.

9 Equity, fair trade and local economy
Inclusive, empowering workplaces with equitable pay; support for local communities and fair trade.

10 Health and happiness
Encouraging active, sociable, meaningful lives to promote good health and well-being.

BioRegional's programme of One Planet Communities

The 'One Planet Communities' programme is one of BioRegional's key initiatives and consists of a network of some of the world's greenest neighbourhoods, where people are apparently living a healthier, higher quality lifestyle using a fair share of the planet's resources.

BioRegional have been working with developers and other stakeholders around the world to plan and develop these neighbourhoods. The Sonoma Mountain Village is an example. The vision is of an 81 hectare, mixed-use, solar-powered, zero-waste community, 40 miles north of San Francisco. The development supports the five-minute lifestyle concept, with parks, shopping, services and a town square all within a short walk of homes and businesses. Community programmes, such as a car- and bike-sharing scheme, walking school buses, neighbourhood electric vehicle shuttles, car-charging stations, community gardening and a daily farmers' market, all create a culture that supports individual lifestyles.

BioRegional's One Planet Living flower
(left)
One Planet Living projects aim to develop solutions for leading happy and healthy lives within the limits of the earth's resources. To do this, projects use a holistic ten-principle sustainability framework that includes:
— Zero carbon
— Zero waste
— Sustainable transport
— Sustainable materials
— Local and sustainable food

4.4
Sustainability is not about single issues

4.4

'I'm not a plastic bag'
(right)
In their book, *Change the World for a Fiver*, activist group We Are What We Do say that every person in the UK uses on average 167 plastic bags a year, that's 10 billion in all. They responded to this fact by approaching handbag designer Anya Hindmarch to create a reusable shopping bag. Anya's bags usually sell for around £500 ($800) but this one sold for £5 ($8), at least initially. It soon became a must-have limited-edition accessory with a much higher resale price.

The term sustainability encapsulates a complex set of ideas. It can embrace almost any aspect of human awareness and responsiveness to ecological and social responsibilities and impacts. Sustainability is therefore difficult to put in a nutshell. As a result, it can be difficult to know how to act in response to a heightened awareness of sustainability. Sustainability is sometimes reduced to single issues, easy-to-grasp principles or actions that make us feel that we are doing something useful and constructive.

These single issues can be dangerous, however, if they distract us from seeing the bigger picture. We run the risk of focusing on a few highly visible, but actually quite minor issues, and failing to address the overall environmental and social impacts of our lifestyles, organizations and neighbourhoods.

Token gestures?
It's not about plastic bags

Plastic carrier bags are a powerful and highly visible symbol of our excessive consumption. In Ireland and other countries, they are no longer automatically given away with every purchase. In the UK, there has been a reaction against the branded plastic carrier bag in the form of the ethical reusable shopping bag.

Plastic carrier bags are considered flimsy and disposable, but due to their material composition they don't go away when we are done with them. Better, surely, to replace them with more robust alternatives made from natural materials?

But is it not even better to try and change the real cause of the problem with plastic carrier bags: the attitudes and behaviour of the people who use and dispose of them so readily?

Replacing one bag with another doesn't address the real underlying issue of our excessive consumption of resources and failure to take responsibility for the full ecological impacts of our lifestyles. Eradicating the plastic carrier bag won't really achieve anything if we simply replace it with an alternative. It could even give us a false sense of achievement and prevent us from going on to look carefully at other aspects of our lifestyles. It makes no sense to use an ethical shopping bag but still fly to the Caribbean for our holidays. Sustainable lifestyles are not just about saying no to plastic bags.

**'I am a plastic bag and
I'm 100% recyclable'**
(left)
The disposability of plastic carrier bags is a consequence of our own wasteful behaviour more than their design. A plastic carrier bag can be reused and recycled over a life cycle much greater than that of a fabric bag. The humble plastic carrier bag can therefore actually be an environmentally considered choice, if we use and reuse it appropriately.

4.5
Types of capital in sustainable development

Pursuing sustainability as a goal involves striving to resolve conflicts between a number of competing agendas and concerns. This involves managing and either maintaining or adding to a number of capitals. The term capital here refers to the stock and the quality of the various natural and human resources available to us; for example the skills, health and knowledge of the population and the quality of the air.

Sustainable development requires our total capital to be non-decreasing. A number of total capital models are receiving considerable attention from governments, businesses, organizations and communities, and form the basis of sustainability measurement tools.

These models recognize the economic dimension of sustainable development (economic sustainability), while recognizing the need to strike a balance between the benefits (and costs) of economic activity, the carrying capacity of our natural environment and issues of social equity.

The Triple Bottom Line

The three pillars of sustainable development can be expressed in terms of three capitals: economic, social and natural capital. The simultaneous pursuit of economic prosperity, environmental quality, and social equity is often referred to as the Triple Bottom Line (3BL). The idea underpinning the 3BL is that a business or enterprise should consider all three of these capitals, and its success should be measured in terms of its social-ethical and environmental, as well as its financial, performance.

Within this model, the three capitals have equal weight and value. This holistic way of assessing performance is helpful to businesses trying to tackle the complex and varied challenges of sustainable development.

The 3BL model was developed with the help of industrialists, as a way of enabling the sustainable development concept to be introduced into the financial accounting and reporting procedures of businesses. It requires that an enterprise be responsible to stakeholders rather than shareholders, and be a vehicle for serving stakeholder interests rather than simply maximizing shareholder profits.

Criticisms of 3BL

A weakness of the 3BL model lies in the difficulty of applying it in a monetary-based economic system. There is no simple way to measure, in monetary terms, specific costs and benefits of impacts on either society or the environment.

The 3BL model gives equal weighting to economic, social and natural capital. Yet the concentric-circle model of sustainable development (see page 83) makes it clear that environmental sustainability is pre-conditional for ongoing economic and social prosperity; the biosphere sets the limits as to what our society and economy can generate and consume.

Triple Bottom Line accounting may even be seen as an attempt by otherwise exploitative corporations to avoid punitive legislation and taxation, by creating a spurious people-friendly and eco-friendly image purely for public relations purposes. As always, it is worth investigating the ecological and social claims of any company and its products very carefully.

The Triple Bottom Line

1 People
Human capital

Human capital relates to fair and beneficial organizational practices in relation to labour, the community and region in which an organization conducts its operations. A Triple Bottom Line (3BL) enterprise seeks to benefit all of its constituencies, and not exploit or endanger any of them. A percentage of profits is returned to the original producers of products and raw materials (fair trade). Exploitative and child labour is not used.

All contracted companies are monitored to ensure they provide a safe working environment, demand tolerable working hours, and pay their workers a fair salary. The enterprise also engages in additional positive activities that actively contribute to community well-being, such as health care provision and education. Evaluating all of this human capital can be highly subjective. For example, child labour may be acceptable in some circumstances, and better than alternative ways of alleviating poverty.

2 Planet
Natural capital

Natural capital refers to sustainable environmental practices. A 3BL enterprise endeavours to curtail its environmental impacts. It will seek to continually reduce its ecological footprint. The enterprise should develop a life-cycle thinking approach in relation to its products and services. A 3BL enterprise does not produce harmful or destructive products such as weapons or toxic chemicals.

3 Profit
Economic capital

A 3BL approach does not simply involve augmenting traditional financial profit-and-loss accounting with a financial valuation of social and environmental impacts. The profits of human and natural capital should also be included as calculable benefits. In this way, the real economic impact of an enterprise can be calculated.

Attempting to quantify human and environmental, as well as financial, capital in terms of a bottom line is a relatively new and still problematic endeavour. It involves trying to put a monetary price on things, such as the biological systems of the earth, which are literally priceless.

The five capitals model

The concept of the Triple Bottom Line is developed in the five capitals model, outlined by Jonathan Porritt in his book *Capitalism as if the World Matters*. With the sustainable development charity Forum for the Future, Porritt suggests that there are five types of sustainable capital from which we derive the goods and services we need to maintain the quality of our lives: natural, human, social, manufactured and financial capital. Sustainability requires that these five capital assets must be managed, and either maintained or added to.

The Five Capitals model sees the crisis of sustainability as arising from the fact that we are consuming our stocks of natural, human and social capital faster than they are being produced and replenished. Unless this rate of consumption is controlled, these vital stocks cannot be sustained in the long-term.

With this in mind, businesses should identify and implement practices that either increase the stocks of these capital assets (living off the income, rather than depleting the capital), or substitute one form of capital for another (but only to a limited extent).

The Five Capitals model attempts to integrate our awareness of the state of the earth and its people with the core tenets of capitalism. It defines sustainability in terms of our collective capacity to maintain and enhance our stocks of natural, social, human, manufactured and financial capital.

Forum for the Future argues that such an alignment of sustainability and capitalism is crucial if we are to harness market-based economics to a recognition of the non-negotiable imperative of fashioning sustainable livelihoods for the six billion people on our planet (which may rise to nine billion by the second half of this century).

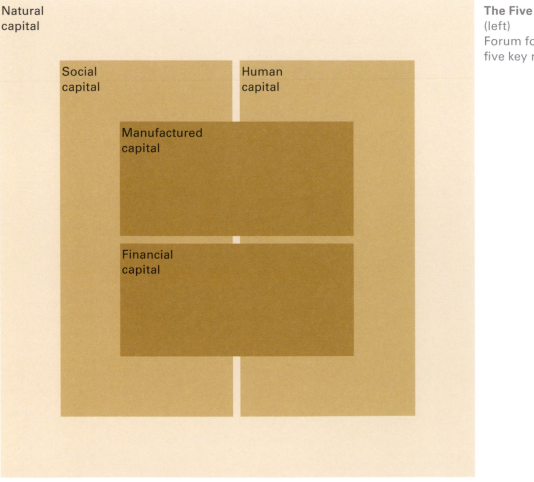

Natural capital

Social capital

Human capital

Manufactured capital

Financial capital

The Five Capitals model
(left)
Forum for the Future's
five key resources.

The Five Capitals model
Forum for the Future's
five key resources

1 Natural capital

Natural capital is any stock or flow
of energy and material within the
environment that produces goods and
services.

2 Human capital

Human capital consists of people's
health, knowledge, skills and
motivation. All these things are needed
for productive work. Enhancing human
capital through education and training
is central to a flourishing economy.

3 Social capital

Social capital is concerned with the
institutions that help us maintain and
develop human capital in partnership
with others; such as families,
communities, businesses, trade unions,
schools and voluntary organizations.

4 Manufacturing capital

Manufacturing capital comprises
material goods or fixed assets that
contribute to the production process
such as tools, machines and buildings.

5 Financial capital

Financial capital plays an important
role in our economy, enabling the
other types of capital to be owned and
traded. Unlike the other types of capital,
it has no real value in itself but is simply
representative of natural, human, social
or manufactured capital.

4.6
Should we use the 'S' word?

"…it can be argued that the statement of these three concerns [the three pillars of sustainability] is simply our modern, secularized way of repeating age-old wisdom teachings that have been expressed down the centuries in the form of mythology and sacred literature. Myths have always existed and will always exist because it is through the metaphorical language of myth that a culture articulates its deepest concerns. Sustainable development can be seen as our own myth, emerging from a culture of science, technology and reason."

Stuart Walker
Sustainable by Design (2006:16)

4.1   4.2   4.3   4.4   4.5   4.6
Should we use
the 'S' word?

96 / 97

The word sustainability had a long life before it was pressed into service by advocates of a need for greater human awareness and responsiveness to ecological and social responsibilities and impacts. Businesses and other organizations talk about their sustainability in terms of their prospects and plans for the future, meaning simply: will they be around in five years time?

Sustainability in the more specialized sense of ecological longevity has recently emerged as a dominant cultural discourse, and a field of academic and professional specialism. Artists, corporations, journalists and politicians are all now engaging with sustainability as an agenda; we have seen the rise of the 'S' word.

But how carefully do we consider what we mean when we use the 'S' word? Sustainability as a term is asked to do a huge amount of work in embracing almost any possible dimension of human awareness and receptiveness to ecological and social responsibilities and impacts. Is this helpful? Is there a danger that we stop interrogating what we mean by the 'S' word because of its complexity, and begin using it lazily as a shorthand term for a huge range of issues that we feel are in some way interconnected?

Sustainability as modern myth

Stuart Walker discusses sustainability as the dominant 'myth' in contemporary industrialized society (see quote opposite). Walker's view is that the idea of sustainable development is our shared cultural way of reinventing values and principles that have been increasingly forgotten in the rapid growth of industrialized modern society.

To view sustainable development as a myth is not to doubt its relevance or validity. Myths are inherited shared stories that help us to understand the world and our place within it. The fact that the term and concept of sustainability has such contemporary cultural value shows the importance we now collectively place on the issues and ideas it represents.

Sustainastic...

Sustainable...

Sustainabulous...

Sustainiferous...

Interview
Jonathon Porritt

Jonathon Porritt
Forum for the Future

Jonathon Porritt is co-founder of Forum for the Future, the UK's leading sustainable development charity. He was formerly director of the environmental campaign group Friends of the Earth (1984–90); co-chair of the UK Green Party (1980–83), of which he is still a member; chairman of the United Nations Environment and Development, UK Committee (1993–96); and a trustee of the UK arm of the World Wildlife Fund Network of environmental organizations (1991–2005). He stood down as chairman of the UK Sustainable Development Commission in July 2009, after nine years advising government ministers.

As someone who's been involved in the environmental debate for several decades now, when do you think the 'S' word, sustainability, became the prominent term used in this debate?

I suppose that its early origins were back in the mid-1970s; the concept of sustainable development was first used by Barbara Ward and the International Institute for Environment and Development (IIED), and then picked-up in the UN's Brundtland report, which had a huge impact. From 1987 onwards, it gradually achieved more visibility in the run-up to the Earth Summit in Rio, in 1992, by which time it was reasonably well-established in terms of the global treaty negotiations around climate change, biodiversity, Agenda 21 and so on. Definitions were reasonably clear by then. However, people use sustainability and sustainable development interchangeably, which isn't terribly helpful, but you can see why they do that.

Sustainability is reasonably well-understood now, so much so that it is massively abused by all sorts of people who use the concept to enable them to bandwagon onto whatever idea it is that they think is in vogue at the time.

Does that concern you?

I'm not that concerned about it. The reality is that ideas only ever get currency if they're used by lots of people in lots of contexts, and sustainable as an adjective in itself is inevitably going to be used by lots of people for lots of purposes. If the adjective sustainable applies to something that can be made to last over time, then clearly there are lots of uses for it that have nothing to do with sustainable development as a political ideology or political concept.

There are critics who question the whole notion of sustainable development itself, who claim that it's nonsensical to talk about development that is sustainable. Where do you stand on that view?

Those people have never really thought about economic development and what it means, and are totally disconnected from any serious consideration about the power and the concept of sustainable development. For people who are worried about poverty in the world today, and for people who know that we live in a miserable world as far as the poorest four or five billion people are concerned, I'm always interested to know what other concept they'd like to talk about, if not sustainable development.

4.1   4.2   4.3   4.4   4.5   4.6
Should we use
the 'S' word?

98 / 99

They presumably agree that we need to make the lives of those people better; well, that requires economic development. We know that if we have the same kind of development that we've had until now, then that's game over for not just the four billion, but humankind as a whole. So you either have *unsustainable* economic development, or you have *sustainable* economic development. It's a complete non-debate to me.

Do you think the concept of sustainable development is understood worldwide; in China and South America, for example?

It's understood a lot more than one might imagine in those countries. In China, for instance, the concept of sustainable development is very well understood; they may not practice it, but they certainly understand it. In America it's problematic, because America is a nation that is not given to understanding the concept of limits, and you can't talk about sustainable development unless you talk about limits. In other developing countries that I've visited, I think they know perfectly well that they're talking about ways of improving the material lot of their population and their people in ways that don't destroy the foundations of wealth for the future, and whether they call that sustainable development or not, that's a pretty clear concept.

In Brazil I've had, over the years, endless discussions with Brazilian activists and politicians which show that they know as much about the practicalities of what sustainable development means as anybody here in the UK.

So in places like the US do we need a different language, perhaps, to talk about these issues, if they're not quite getting it?

Possibly. There comes a point where you've got to say the language isn't really the deal. The issue in America is not really the language; the issue in America is that they are philosophically disinclined to accept the realities of humankind. Culturally, it seems almost impossible for Americans to understand that this is a bounded planet with limited resources, and we have to constrain the impact of our economy within those limits. I'm speaking very, very generally here. There are millions of Americans who understand that only too well, but if you look at the dominant culture, dominant *political* culture in particular, this is a concept that it still deeply unwelcome. They're all still playing through one version or another of the American dream, and no one has really made it clear that the American Dream for the 21st century is going to have to look very different.

Do you think the sustainability debate is further on in Europe than in North America?

Yes, a long way.

And how much do you think that might be connected to politics, the political landscape of Europe?

I think for a lot of European countries — especially Scandinavia, Germany, Benelux — trying to get the right balance between economic development, well-being and biophysical sustainability is pretty old hat. So if you call that kind of compact — about well-being, justice, development and environment — sustainable development, then it makes a lot of sense, and certainly the European economies have been seeking to find that kind of balance for a long time.

We're seeing a rise in the profile of political parties with a green agenda. Do you think these have to be careful in the language they use in trying to communicate to a broader audience?

The UK Green Party has always talked primarily about social justice and economics. You can only address the environment as a policy area, if you like, if you've sorted out issues of economics, justice and governance.

I think that people will eventually understand that the precondition of doing anything good in anybody's life is understanding our relationship with the rest of life on earth, and that is in essence a set of green constructs, understanding how we need to work within the earth's natural limits.

Forum for the Future logotype
(left)
Jonathon Porritt is founder director of Forum for the Future, the UK's leading sustainable development non-governmental organization (NGO). It works internationally with government, business and public service providers, helping them to develop strategies to achieve success through sustainability, to deliver products and services which enhance people's lives and are better for the environment, and to lead the way to a better world.

Part III
Design for sustainable change

Part III explores ways in which design and sustainability interrelate. If design is a key element of the contemporary focus on improved sustainability, how is this happening? In what ways is design intervening in and driving sustainable change? The sustainability agenda asks fundamental questions of design.

The following chapters explore current understandings of how design relates to the core facets of sustainability, how the sustainability agenda is changing the roles and responsibilities of design and designers and finally how designers are taking action, all demonstrated through recent real-life examples.

We need to acknowledge that the design community is becoming increasingly conscious of sustainable design, but that progress can differ across different design sectors and professions. The words design and sustainability are not fixed in their meaning and neither is the emerging language of design for sustainability.

Chapter 5
Sustainability
and design

5.0

Design is critical in addressing the various agendas of sustainability, because it can have significant (both positive and negative) economic, environmental and social ripple effects. Design can drive the dematerialization of products, processes, and services. More importantly, design can change our attitudes and behaviours. When starting to think about designing for sustainable change, designers need to be aware of the different ways they can begin to consider sustainability, its key issues and its evolving narratives.

The recent history of environmentally and socially considered design can be told through the language that has been used to describe it. There has been a succession of terms, from green design, to ecodesign to sustainable design (or design for sustainability, sometimes abbreviated to 'DfS') to describe the context and current thinking on how design is responding to sustainable development agendas. These terms may often seem interchangeable and the differences between them are not always obvious. But this development in terminology represents an increasing sophistication in our thinking about environmentally and socially considered design. If we use these terms interchangeably, without considering the real differences they signify, then we fail to appreciate the development in our understanding of how design and sustainability interrelate.

Part III
Design for
sustainable
change

Chapter 5
Sustainability
and design

5.1
Green design:
a single-issues
approach

The waste management hierarchy
(right)
Also known as the three Rs, this model
usefully shows the preferred sequence
in which we should consider different
approaches to dealing with the issue
of waste: reduce, reuse and recycle.
Disposal is a last resort.

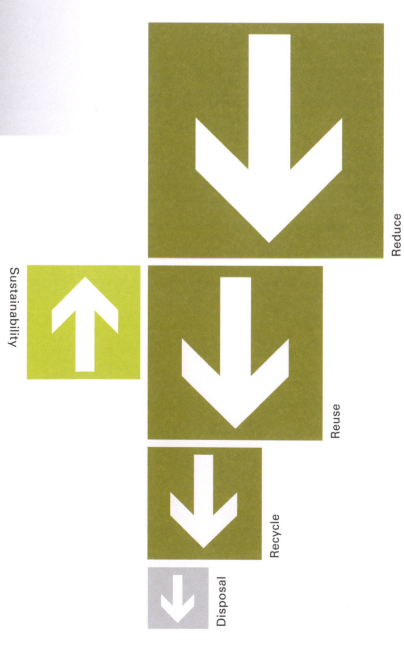

Sustainability

Reduce

Reuse

Recycle

Disposal

The term green design was the first to be used by the design community as they became aware of environmental considerations in the early 1990s. Green design has come to mean a focus on single issues, or one aspect of a design's ecological impact; for example materials or energy consumption. For many designers, their way into the practice of environmentally considered design is through the use of recycled materials. Substituting a virgin polymer with a recycled alternative can be a simple and often very visible way of addressing environmental impact, without challenging or significantly altering a product's purpose or form.

Recycled design

Many designers, especially designer-makers, embrace the aesthetic properties and possibilities of using recycled materials and products in their practice. This is often what might be called recycled design. An aesthetic of recycling, in which the first origin of the material is clear to see in the new design, can be powerful in communicating environmental awareness. Recycled design is, however, often difficult to do on a large scale. It is also essentially reactive, in that it responds to (and even encourages the continuation of) existing material waste streams. Waste can be seen as a design flaw, but this should not be approached only through material recycling.

Designers often begin with materials, and design through materials. Material recycling is therefore a natural instinct for a designer seeking to reduce environmental impacts. Yet as a design strategy, using recycled materials is not always environmentally beneficial, particularly when a product has not been designed for recycling or with end-of-life in mind.

Remarkable Pencils Ltd

Remarkable Pencils Ltd began with the design and manufacture of pencils from recycled polystyrene vending cups. The company went on to produce a wide range of recycled stationery products, with a strong commitment to promoting recycling to its consumers.

Remarkable has since broadened its collection of promotional products, and all are now made either in the UK, from UK recycled waste, certified by the Forestry Stewardship Council, or from organic materials. The original Remarkable recycled pencil however remains the company's iconic product, and is an example of single-issue, environmentally considered design focusing solely on materials. This green design approach involves substituting one material for another within an existing product.

The remarkable recycled pencil
(above)
Remarkable turn used polystyrene vending cups into pencils. Each pencil is made from approximately one recycled cup. In its early years, the company focused exclusively on the use of recycled materials in stationery products. Remarkable is no longer just about recycling, and now produces a broader range of promotional products with a wider range of environmental credentials.

"Environmentally sound materials do not exist; environmentally friendly design approaches do."

John Thackara
In the Bubble: Designing in a Complex World (2005:14)

Part III
Design for
sustainable
change

Chapter 5
Sustainability
and design

5.2
Ecodesign:
life-cycle thinking

Ecodesign moves beyond a focus on a single aspect of a product's ecological impact, to consider the whole product life cycle. A product in this sense could be a garment, an electrical device, a piece of furniture or an item of printed literature. Ecodesign takes a holistic view of where designers should focus in seeking to reduce the environmental impacts of a product in its manufacture and consumption.

The greatest environmental impact of an electrical product over its lifetime is likely to be in the use phase; it therefore makes sense for the designer to focus on this part of the product life cycle before considering, for example, manufacture. Considering the whole life cycle of a product ensures the designer is aware of all the environmental issues associated with a design outcome. The designer then knows where to focus to minimize environmental impacts. If design outcomes are to have little negative overall impact, then the designer needs to consider the many potential impacts throughout the entire life cycle. This means considering how the design interacts with the environment during material extraction and production, manufacture, use and at end-of-life. Transportation between these phases may also have a significant environmental impact.

Ecodesign is an evolutionary approach that integrates environmental considerations into existing design practices. The key ideas are design modification and pragmatism. Existing design processes are used as the starting point.

"Ecodesign addresses all environmental impacts of a product throughout the complete life cycle of the product, whilst aiming to enhance other criteria like function, quality, and appearance."

Philip Goggin
Glossary: Key concepts and definitions,
co-design (1996:5–6)

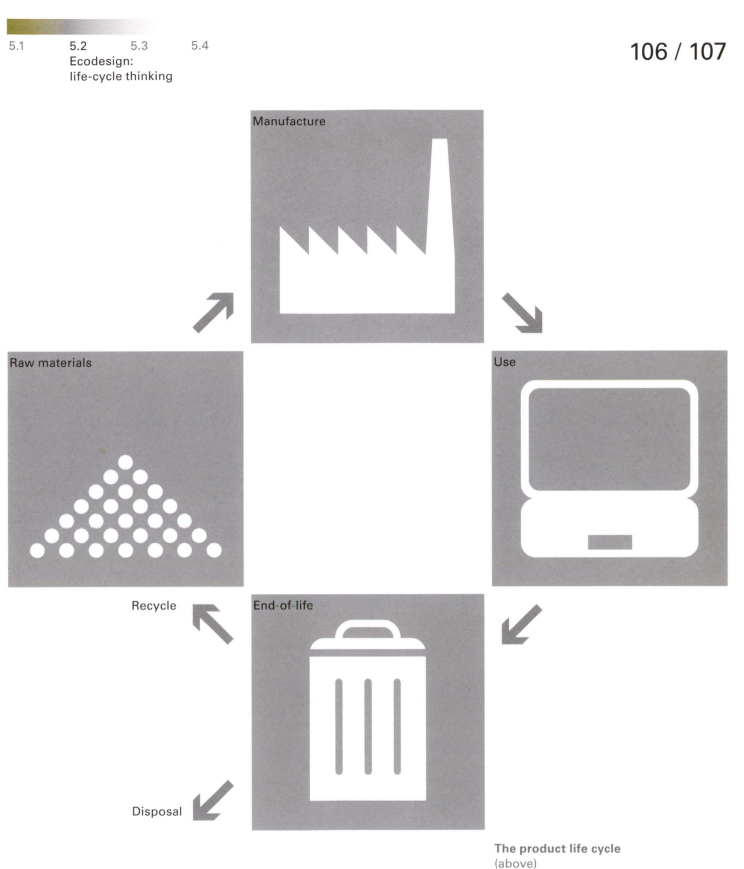

Manufacture

Use

Raw materials

Recycle   End-of-life

Disposal

The product life cycle
(above)
'Ecodesign' considers environmental
impacts during the whole product life
cycle, from extraction of raw materials,
to product manufacture, to product
use and finally to treatment at end-
of-life. The environmental impacts of
transportation between these phases
of the life cycle are also considered.
Globalized manufacturing means that
even an apparently simple product may
contain components from many parts
of the world.

Part III
Design for
sustainable
change

Chapter 5
Sustainability
and design

Life cycle methods and tools

Each stage of the product life cycle has potential human and environmental impacts. Making informed decisions can therefore be difficult. Designers need reliable and useful data on the relative impacts of all materials and processes relating to the product they are designing.

Life cycle assessment (LCA) is a method of measuring the relative human and environmental impacts of products across their full life cycle. LCA allows designers to make informed decisions on where the greatest impacts are, and the design strategies that can be used to design out those impacts. There are a number of methods and tools that can help designers to adopt life cycle thinking. These are most commonly used by product and industrial designers and engineers.

Life cycle assessment tools

Comparisons of environmental impacts between different phases of the product life cycle are made possible by LCA tools. These tools range from relatively inexpensive online devices to more complex and costly tools used by larger organizations. These are computer-based calculators into which we enter a wide range of numerical data about the product life cycle in order to work out the points at which we can most usefully intervene as designers.

It is important to recognize that while the calculations of LCA tools are based on numerical data, the comparisons they generate are based on variable value-judgements as to the relative importance and equivalence of different types of environmental impact, for example carbon dioxide emissions and water pollution. LCA tools are also essentially retrospective, in that they can only give a detailed picture of a product's life cycle once it is complete. Simplified versions of LCA tools are therefore used to indicate approximate relative environmental impacts across the product life cycle at the start of the design process.

Simplified LCA tools

A comprehensive LCA, combined with user feedback, can offer valuable insights for designers, and increase the credibility of any environmental claims for a product. A full LCA is a very useful technique for marrying systems thinking with design, but can be extremely time consuming and complex. While a full LCA is often not practical in the high-speed design and development process, a number of simplified alternatives exist that allow designs to be assessed and compared quickly and easily.

A simplified LCA enables a designer to see and understand some environmental impacts of design choices, at a more modest cost. Simplified LCA tools allow a quick assessment of the key environmental impacts of a proposed design. This still enables the largest environmental impacts to be identified and used as the focus for a product redesign.

Another cost- and time-effective approach is a simple review of material alternatives. While less comprehensive than even a simplified LCA, this method can help designers to roughly understand and assess the impacts of their design choices. It represents the minimum level of impact assessment that an eco-designer should undertake.

5.1   **5.2**   5.3   5.4
Ecodesign:
life-cycle thinking

108 / 109

From efficiency to effectiveness

Resource efficiency can be a good starting point when thinking about ecodesign. Designers can look for opportunities to reduce material and energy used throughout the life cycle of a product. By doing so, it is possible to not only reduce the environmental impact of a design, but also to reduce costs. This can be a particularly persuasive selling point for sceptical clients or management.

The development of our thinking in relation to environmentally and socially considered design can be characterized as an increasing shift from efficiency to effectiveness. Redesigning a product so that it uses less energy, or less harmful materials, might be considered tweaky ecodesign. Pursuing greater eco-efficiency is often very valuable, especially in the case of products made in large volumes, but is focused on fine-tuning the existing production system to make its impact slightly less negative.

This is designing that accepts the constraints imposed by the current way of making things. As a result, the potential environmental (and social) transformations possible from this kind of approach are often limited.

A more ambitious approach is to seek to move from eco-*efficiency* to eco-*effectiveness*. Being *efficient* is about doing something well (and getting the most out of the resources used) without necessarily questioning the purpose or value of what it is we are doing. Being *effective* is about doing the right thing well, and being prepared to question and ultimately change what we are working towards.

Sustainable Minds
(left)
Sustainable Minds is an online LCA tool that enables rapid iteration and evaluation of product concepts during the design process. Once life cycle data has been entered, the results are broken down into easy-to-read charts. These provide a quick idea of where the main impacts are in the product's life cycle. The various environmental impacts are aggregated into a single number to simplify the results and provide clear information on which to act. The user can input data for several design concepts and visually compare the impacts of any two side by side. Sustainable Minds also has a section providing guidance on ecodesign strategies that may help to reduce the impacts revealed by the software.

Part III
Design for
sustainable
change

Chapter 5
Sustainability
and design

Case study
The Cradle to Cradle design protocol

The Cradle to Cradle design protocol is a model for moving from eco-efficiency to eco-effectiveness in design and manufacture. It has been hugely influential on the thinking of many designers since the protocol was published in William McDonough and Michael Braungart's *Cradle to Cradle: Remaking the Way We Make Things* in 2002. The book sets out a theoretical basis for managing material cycles so that natural materials (biological nutrients) and synthetic materials (technical nutrients) are kept apart to allow for effective material reprocessing and reuse. *Cradle to Cradle*'s authors have implemented their model with a number of leading manufacturers, redesigning not just the products but also the production processes used to make them.

Inspired by nature?

The Cradle to Cradle design protocol is an example of biomimicry, or design that mimics nature. Natural ecosystems are supremely effective in maintaining balance between their constituent elements. Yet natural systems, in contrast to human technologies, evolve over very long periods of time. Human technological development tends to be revolutionary rather than evolutionary. Can we ever create an industrial ecology (in which the waste from one process becomes the food for another) that truly mimics a natural ecosystem such as a forest?

Cradle to Cradle focuses on material cycles. It neglects the issue of energy, except to say that we should harvest solar income in the same way we see in nature. Neither does the protocol address the social dimension of sustainability, focusing instead on environmental considerations of design and manufacture.

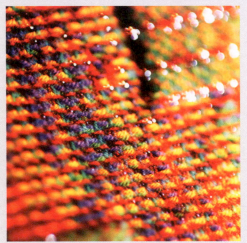

From cradle to grave to Cradle to Cradle
(above and right)
A materials economy based on 'take – make – waste' is replaced by one which mimics the nutrient cycles found in the non-human natural world. The authors of the Cradle to Cradle design protocol claim that this is an example of restorative manufacture. The product itself and the emissions from its production are entirely benign, with no harmful by-products or pollution.

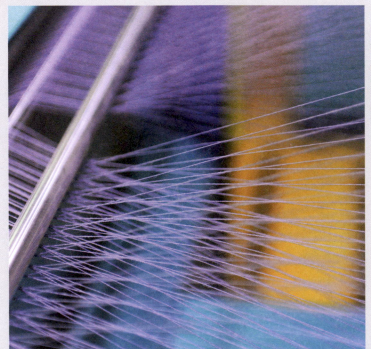

Case study
Herman Miller

Herman Miller Inc. is a worldwide manufacturer of office furniture, known particularly for its range of iconic office chairs. The company's chair designs seek to combine excellent ergonomics and functionality with environmentally considered design.

Herman Miller is often recognized for its environmental efforts such as reduction of packaging, active pollution prevention and green building certification, and is repeatedly listed on the Dow Jones Sustainability World Index. The company credits its 40-year-old participatory management tradition as key to its environmental successes.

The ultimate chair?
(below)
The Embody chair is designed for a cradle to cradle materials cycle, so its materials can be perpetually circulated in closed loops. Keeping materials in a closed-loop system maximizes their value without damaging ecosystems. The chair is designed using 42 per cent recycled content, and is 95 per cent recyclable at the end of its useful life. It has a warranty for 12 years, based on 24-hour use.

Part III
Design for
sustainable
change

Chapter 5
Sustainability
and design

5.3
Corporate social responsibility (CSR) and design

"[CSR is] …the continuing commitment by business to behave ethically and contribute to economic development while improving the quality of life of the workforce and their families as well as the local community and society at large."

Richard Holme and Phil Watts
Corporate Social Responsibility: Making Good Business Sense (2000:8)

Corporate social responsibility (CSR) is the voluntary ethical behaviour of a company towards society, including but not confined to its own shareholders and stakeholders. When embraced fully, CSR does not focus on any one single issue, but identifies employee and wider human rights, environmental protection, community involvement, and supplier relations as core corporate values. Related terms include social responsibility in business, corporate responsibility, corporate citizenship, sustainability and corporate governance. CSR is a common term in Europe, while in the US business ethics is preferred.

For many in the US, the term corporate social responsibility suggests an anti-business agenda imposed upon corporations by those outside the system. Europeans, conversely, can consider the term business ethics to have a moralizing tone, at odds with the corporate view.

Corporate social responsibility took off in the late 1990s, as a tactic employed by large companies seeking to defend themselves against anti-globalization and anti-capitalist protests. CSR has since grown into a more positive agenda by which companies willingly embrace their environmental, community and workforce responsibilities.

In the US, CSR has generally followed a philanthropic model. Companies first focus on making profits, hindered only by their duty to pay taxes. They then donate a share of their profits to charitable causes. On this model, the act of corporate giving would be tainted if the company were to receive any benefit from its donation, such as favourable publicity. The European model of CSR is much more focused on operating the core business in a socially responsible way, complemented by investment in communities for solid business reasons. Clearly, there is no one size fits all approach to CSR internationally, reflecting differing business and cultural values.

A growing number of companies are embracing CSR and using it to differentiate themselves in the marketplace. In these cases, design has an important role in translating CSR principles into tangible actions. This means considering not just the direct environmental and social impacts of a company's products, environments, services and systems, but addressing wider issues such as social inclusion, health, education and crime through design thinking. Design can deliver this new contract between business and society by more effectively and equitably delivering products and services and communicating these achievements and a company's values.

Case study
Interface

Interface is a worldwide manufacturer of carpet tiles and floor coverings. Since the mid-1990s, the company has also been a global pioneer of sustainability led business, with a goal of achieving a zero environmental footprint by the year 2020. This Mission Zero goal applies to every activity and division within the company. The company's strategic commitment to sustainability is credited to its chief executive Ray Anderson, who argues for moving towards a sustainable society through more sustainable business practices.

In delivering its plan, Interface sees itself as climbing the 'seven faces of Mount Sustainability':

1 Moving towards zero waste.

2 Making emissions benign.

3 Using renewable energy.

4 Instigating closed-loop recycling, imitating nature's way of turning waste into food.

5 Ensuring all transportation is resource-efficient.

6 Creating a corporate ecosystem, with cooperation as its founding principle.

7 Assessing costs accurately in order to set real prices.

Product service systems

Interface has pioneered the leasing, rather than sale, of flooring tiles for commercial premises. The company effectively sells the use of its products, and keeps ownership of them throughout the time they are in use at the customer's premises. This requires new product distribution and payment systems, as well as a new kind of relationship between the company and its customers. Leasing typically reduces the amount of products used, but puts greater stresses on those products. Use of a leasing model has seen the company invest in innovations in carpet technology, to make recovered carpet tiles easier to reuse, remanufacture and recycle at the end of their initial useful life cycle.

Interface's leasing model is an example of a Product Service System (PSS), a particular type of systems thinking. Use of a PSS requires a reconsideration of the way in which a manufacturer sells its product, and uncouples commercial success from the usual measure of how many products it can sell. Interface makes money from providing additional *services* rather than selling more *products*, showing that economic value can be created while simultaneously reducing environmental impact.

Systems: lease not own
(left)
Interface has pioneered the leasing, rather than sale, of floor coverings for commercial premises. Carpet is sold as a service, not a product. In return for a monthly leasing charge, the company supplies, installs and replaces its coverings (often tiles) as needed.

This gives the customer more flexibility while allowing the manufacturer to optimize the product life cycle by retaining ownership of it throughout its life. Each tile in the Transformation collection is unique, and maintains a randomness of pattern however it is laid, lending itself to easy replacement.

Part III
Design for
sustainable
change

Chapter 5
Sustainability
and design

5.4
Design for sustainability: radical innovations

Marks & Spencer's Plan A
(right)
Corporate social responsibility (CSR), when embraced fully and convincingly and then successfully communicated to customers, can differentiate a company in the marketplace. CSR constitutes a new form of contract between business and society, often delivered through design. The leading UK retailer Marks & Spencer launched its Plan A (tag line 'there is no Plan B') in January 2007, setting out 100 sustainability related commitments to achieve in five years, with the ultimate goal of becoming the world's most sustainable major retailer.

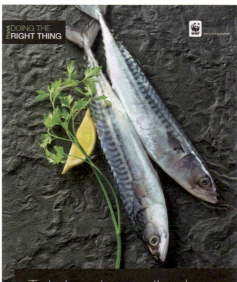

The idea of sustainable design derives directly from that of sustainable development. But might the alternative phrase design for sustainability be better? The term sustainable design suggests we are concerned with sustaining design in and of itself, whereas we are actually concerned with the application of design in pursuit of sustainability. The title of this book (*Design for Sustainable Change*) reflects this emphasis on design as a means to an end, rather than as the end in itself.

The dominant conversation on how design can address sustainable development initially grew out of the environmental life-cycle thinking of ecodesign. To this has now been added a consideration of the social aspects of production and consumption. We have progressed from sustainable product-service systems thinking to an exploration of new ways of living, and a consideration of how design interventions can direct us as citizens (not just consumers) onto a more sustainable path.

This more radical way of thinking does not begin with the idea of a product solution in mind. From the start, it considers the need a product satisfies (such as the need for warmth) and considers if that need could be met in another more sustainable way. The best design outcome may not be a new product, but a new system or mode of product use. For example, car share systems reconfigure the perception that we as consumers need a new car; when what we really need is access to transport. This requires designers to work in a new, more interdisciplinary way. It also requires a more participatory way of working, which involves both target users and anyone else who is influenced, either directly or indirectly, by the design decisions made.

Current definitions and discourses of sustainable design are still predominantly framed within the sustainable production and consumption theme within a market-based economy. New terms such as socially conscious design, design for development and design altruism have emerged to challenge this discourse.

These alternative modes of design are articulated by a small but growing number of designers and architects, often via the World Wide Web, whose priority is to use design to improve the quality of life and opportunities available to the unacceptably large percentage of the world's population who currently live on less than $2 a day. The ideal, sustainable society would be one in which everyone has the same opportunities to live well, within the limits of a supportable environmental footprint. This conception of a sustainable society is simple and clear but problematic. Yet over the past twenty years a growing number of designers and design thinkers have begun to develop visions and proposals for this kind of sustainable society. The design community is beginning to progress towards a better understanding of what it can do to address sustainability agendas, and how it can effectively respond through design.

"[Design for sustainability is] theories and practices for design that cultivate ecological, economic and cultural conditions that will support human well-being indefinitely."

Ann Thorpe
The Designer's Atlas of Sustainability,
(2007:13)

Part III
Design for
sustainable
change

Chapter 5
Sustainability
and design

good
do ~~sustainable~~
design

The 'S' word revisited: is sustainable design just good design?

This book explores the ways in which design and sustainability interrelate. It is not intended to be a niche book on sustainable design or design for sustainability. Once we begin to use these kinds of labels, we risk accepting their underlying concepts uncritically, and treating them as somehow *other* from regular or mainstream design. Is sustainable design just good design? Ideally, yes. Good design should by definition also be sustainable design, but this isn't always the case. This is why it is useful to use special terminology to highlight the fact that much design is currently *unsustainable*.

In this sense there is nothing new about sustainable design, we are just using new language to remind ourselves that all design should be sustainable in order for us to consider it good design.

Dieter Rams' ten principles for product-based design (listed below) embody many ideas that would be recognized by the eco-designer. So why do we need to use the term ecodesign, or the 'S' word? We need the new language of design for sustainability to remind ourselves that design must be sustainable to be *good* design, something that has been forgotten by many designers, until recently. When all design is sustainable, then we no longer need to use the language of sustainable design.

Dieter Rams' ten principles for good design
(right)
In the early 1980s, the celebrated product and furniture designer Dieter Rams asked himself the question 'Is my design good design?' This led him to formulate his ten principles for good design.[1]

Good design is innovative.

Good design makes a product useful.

Good design is aesthetic.

Good design makes a product understandable.

Good design is unobtrusive.

Good design is honest.

Good design is long-lasting.

Good design is thorough down to the last detail.

Good design is environmentally friendly.

Good design is as little design as possible.

[1] Kemp & Ueki-Polet (2010)

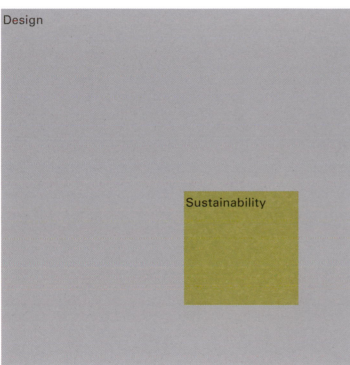

**From sustainability in design to
design in sustainability**
(above)
Sustainability should not be just an
add-on to the design that we do; it
must be integral to that design, and
define that design in terms of its goals
and ambitions. Rather than thinking of
sustainability as sitting within design,
we must think of design as sitting within
sustainability. Sustainability must define
our world view, and everything we
design should contribute to delivering
that sustainable world view. Good design
serves a sustainable world view.

Chapter 6
Design for
sustainable
living

6.0

This chapter examines the different levels at which we might focus in seeking to bring about design for sustainable change: individual behaviour in the home; use of product service systems; participation in shared public services; fundamental lifestyle choices about where and how to live; and the planning of sustainable towns, cities and regions.

Sustainable lifestyles for the masses are only achievable collectively, as the result of cooperation and systems-level thinking. The sustainability agenda does not require us to become hermits, living in isolation from one another. Rather, it demands that we seek out and exploit the benefits of collaboration and social organization. A more sustainable future is a shared future. Design for sustainable living recognizes and celebrates our social nature.

Part III
Design for
sustainable
change

Chapter 6
Design for
sustainable
living

6.1
Designing
sustainable
behaviour

**DIY Kyoto's Wattson energy meter:
making energy saving easier**
(right)

Energy meters, such as the Wattson, measure the electricity being consumed in your home at any moment. The display shows how much electricity your home is using, either in units of electricity (watts) or financial cost per year at the current rate of consumption. The idea is that once you see how much energy you are using, you have an incentive to reduce your consumption, for example by switching off devices you aren't actually using. DIY Kyoto claims that people using Wattson save on average 20 per cent on their household energy bills. The Wattson is designed to be stylish enough to fit in with the decor of a modern living room, rather than be locked away in a cupboard.

Designing for sustainability is not just about the design of products and services. It is also about how we use those products and services and our patterns of behaviour. Rebound effects can occur when we are presented with a more eco-efficient product, such as a low-energy light bulb. If the bulb uses half as much energy as the old bulb it replaces, then we might be tempted to think we no longer need to worry about turning it off when we have finished using it, thereby undermining the potential benefit. The disposable plastic carrier bag is only made disposable by our discarding it after a single use. The bag's apparent disposability is not unavoidably designed in; we could continue to use the same bag for a year, if we take care of it and remember to reuse it.

Making sustainable actions easy

The key to designing for sustainable behaviour can be making sustainable actions easy and fitting them into existing patterns of behaviour. In this way, sustainable behaviour becomes invisible to people and does not require them to make conscious or deliberate decisions to do things differently to how they intended. This approach normalizes sustainability, so that it becomes what we do without having to think too hard about it.

Awareness and incentive

Another approach to designing for sustainable behaviour is to make people aware of their current unsustainable behaviour and present them with an incentive to change that behaviour. Energy use in the home is often excessive; we all leave electrical appliances switched on (or on standby) that are not being used. Rising energy costs also make this wasteful behaviour increasingly expensive.

Domestic energy meters respond to this behaviour by displaying the electricity being consumed in the home at any moment. Once we see how much energy we are using, we have an incentive to reduce consumption. Often we are unaware that our actions are wasteful, or we may feel locked in to certain ways of doing things, just because that's the way we've always done them. Breaking these patterns of behaviour is just as much a challenge to the designer as improving product eco-efficiency.

Use, not own

Many products that we own, we may really only need to use a few times a year. For example, an electric garden hedge trimmer is only needed in the summer months, and often lays dormant in a shed or garage in winter. Even in summer we will only use it a few times. The same is often the case with power tools; we may only use an electric drill to put up shelves. For these products of infrequent use, what we really want is availability rather than ownership. We could quite easily share them with other users without affecting their availability to us when we want them. Owning a product often has associated burdens, such as value depreciation and maintenance costs, which are removed when we switch to a use, not own model.

Having access to products as and when we need them, but without actually owning them, is the customer experience of product service systems (see page 113). Interface sells carpet as a service, not a product. In return for a monthly leasing charge, the company supplies, installs and replaces its floor coverings as needed, giving the customer more flexibility. Product service systems of this kind are often more ecologically efficient than product ownership and take a systems-view to designing more sustainable user behaviour.

The environmental benefits associated with maximizing product use and life in a PSS model must, however, be balanced against the impacts arising from increased transportation of products between users. Like any strategy with the potential to yield environmental savings, PSS are not always better as a matter of course, but should be considered on a case-by-case basis.

Purchasing performance

In many cases, what we actually want to purchase is performance (moving, cooling, message taking, clothes washing) rather than the product that delivers that performance. Shared ownership or leasing can give us access to products when we need them, without the burdens of ownership. Delivered via a PSS model, this can mean fewer products and increased resource productivity. Products may need to be redesigned to withstand more intense use. It is also in the manufacturer's interest to extend the life of its products as much as possible, for example through repair and refurbishment. Ideally, a product will only be replaced when it has reached the end of its functional life, or perhaps been superseded by a more efficient design. The user benefits by having access to a range of products, via the supplier, and so can better meet his or her changing needs without the burden or expense of owning lots of products, some of which may be rarely used.

Part III
Design for
sustainable
change

Chapter 6
Design for
sustainable
living

6.2
Designing sustainable systems

Product redesign can be a valuable environmental strategy, especially in the case of products made in large volumes. But the benefits of what might be considered tweaky ecodesign may be limited if wider systems of product use are not considered. Product service systems (PSS) deliver benefit and utility to their users through a focused provision of products within an intelligently designed system. The system, not the product, becomes the primary focus for the designer. Indeed, many PSS succeed simply by making existing products available to users in new and better ways. Environmental savings can be gained from reconsidering how we use products, without necessarily redesigning the products themselves.

Sustainable systems design shares its core principle with service design and examples of successful service design, such as Streetcar (see pages 44–45), are based on a systems-design approach. The improved functionality of sustainable systems comes from the fact that they encourage more sustainable patterns of user behaviour. They make it easy for us to act more sustainably, by taking away the frustrations of trying to use products or perform individual actions that don't integrate into a wider supporting system. Owning an electric car, with its potentially reduced greenhouse gas emissions, is only a viable choice where there is an adequate supporting system of convenient charging points to facilitate that use.

In this way, systems design, like service design, often requires the integration of many different elements, and the cooperation of many participants. A sustainable system is also only as good as its weakest part; systems-thinking requires a holistic perspective. While the benefits are potentially far greater, systems design is also much more challenging than product redesign.

Case study
Vélib' cycle hire scheme

Vélib' (short for *vélo libre* or *vélo liberté*) is a self-service bicycle hire scheme in Paris, France. As a subscriber to the scheme, you can collect a bike from any of the rental stations in the city and return it to any other station. The several hundred stations are sited every 300 metres within the area covered, and thousands of bikes are available 24 hours a day. The hire scheme integrates with an extensive network of cycle lanes in the city, ensuring safety. Since its inception, the Vélib' scheme has been extended outwards from the city centre, making it the largest system of its kind in the world.

Vélib' is a classic example of systems design, comprising a network of carefully sited rental stations around Paris, integrated through electronic communications. Yet the scheme also incorporates many elements of more traditional product and communication design. The bikes themselves are designed to withstand intensive use, as they need to be used safely by large numbers of people. They are also designed to withstand abuse; as such schemes are prone to vandalism and theft.

The bikes use non-standard components to discourage cannibalization of their parts by bike owners, and their working mechanisms are enclosed to reduce the need for maintenance. The bikes are also very distinctive in appearance, so discouraging theft.

Predicting and serving demand is clearly a challenge for this type of scheme. Preliminary research can only ever suggest likely demand for a service, and so the logistics of ensuring that bikes are available where and when people want them can involve redistributing bikes between stations during the day.

Providing the infrastructure of a bike hire scheme, in the form of bike stations and cycle routes, is not in itself enough. People have to be persuaded that the scheme can work for them, and so promotion is key, as is getting the pricing right; the scheme must be economical to use in comparison to other available modes of transport. Such hire schemes are often aimed at non-habitual cyclists, who don't already own a bike. Providing training in how to cycle safely in the city is also vital to the success of any scheme seeking to encourage safe, sustainable personal urban transport.

Vélib' cycle hire scheme
(left)
Vélib' is a self-service bicycle hire scheme in Paris, France. Such schemes are becoming increasingly common in cities, as governing authorities seek to encourage more sustainable modes of personal transport, to reduce road congestion and promote personal health and well-being.

Part III
Design for
sustainable
change

Chapter 6
Design for
sustainable
living

6.3 Designing sustainable lifestyles

"Sustainable living can be defined as a lifestyle that aims to operate without exhausting any natural resources or challenging any ethical considerations and the development of a sustainable lifestyle addresses the key human needs of housing, clothing, food, health care, education, energy, transport and leisure."

Andrew Darnton
Driving Public Behaviours for Sustainable Lifestyles,
(2004:Report 2:6)

Lifestyles are about how we organize and direct our lives, and how we interact with one another in the decisions and choices we make. Our lifestyles are partly defined by our patterns of consumption. Consumption choices might fulfil our needs and aspirations, but they also have a major impact on our environments, societies and markets. Moving towards a sustainable lifestyle therefore means progressively minimizing our consumption of the Earth's natural resources (for example, reducing our levels of energy use, pollution and waste) and the social injustices connected to the goods and services we consume.

Lifestyles are also shaped by other factors. Lifestyles are not just individual, they are communal; their roots are in culture, politics, economics and social norms. For sustainable lifestyles to become the norm, all of these levels of influence must be considered.

The role of design

Design and designers have an important role to play in exploring opportunities for the development of lifestyle choices that allow individuals to meet their needs and aspirations, while also taking into account environmental and social impacts. Design can help us to rethink our consumer purchasing behaviours and the ways in which we organize our everyday lives.

This can mean refocusing design away from the conventional designer-client relationship. The Young Foundation views social innovation as 'innovative activities and services that are motivated by the goal of meeting a social need and that are predominantly developed and diffused through organizations whose primary purposes are social'.[1] Design and designers can translate this ideal into practical, pragmatic and people-orientated solutions. If design is to drive social innovation in this way, then the clients of design are increasingly likely to become government agencies, non-governmental organizations (NGOs) and community organizations. This opens up many new opportunities for design and designers, and could lead designers to increasingly question their role within current business models.

This is already happening, as national and international policy makers, non-profit organizations and progressive corporations are recognizing the role of design in moving us towards sustainable lifestyles.

Sustainable lifestyles are not, then, just a matter of consumer behaviour. Sustainable patterns of living derive from innovative and appropriate solutions to local challenges. The notion of sustainable lifestyle should not therefore be misunderstood as being just a rich nation's choice. The desire to enjoy Western living standards is clearly very strong in developing countries. These countries, however, also have many sustainable solutions to offer already, some of which it may be possible to translate into the context of the developed world. This is a field requiring careful exploration and understanding, as we seek to develop innovative ways of designing sustainable lifestyle solutions in different parts of the world.

[1] Mulgan (2007:8)

Part III
Design for
sustainable
change

Chapter 6
Design for
sustainable
living

Case study
The Beddington Zero Energy Development (BedZED)

The Beddington Zero Energy Development (BedZED), designed by Bill Dunster and ZEDfactory Architects, is the UK's largest mixed-use sustainable community. It was designed to create a thriving community in which ordinary people could enjoy a high quality of life, without using more than their fair share of the Earth's resources. BedZED was initiated by the sustainable development charity BioRegional and architects ZEDfactory, and was funded by Peabody Trust housing association. It was completed and occupied in 2002, and comprises 50 per cent housing for sale, 25 per cent 'key worker' shared ownership and 25 per cent social housing for rent.

People move to BedZED with typical developed-world lifestyles, characterized by over consumption of resources and high ecological impact. BioRegional have demonstrated that BedZED residents are able to change their lifestyles and behaviours significantly for the better through living there.

The holistic design of BedZED, and the services available to its residents, prompt this lifestyle change on three levels:

1 The passive design creates low heating and water usage by residents; homes are carefully positioned and so well insulated that additional heating is rarely required.

2 The design and services allow residents to make sustainable behavioural choices; car driving is effectively designed out of residents' routines by the site's location and the availability of public transport.

3 The BedZED community has created its own facilities and groups to improve their quality of life and reduce their environmental impacts.

Beddington Zero Energy Development (BedZED)
(right)
BedZED is located on an ex-brownfield site, close to existing road and rail travel connections. The development's sustainability credentials are communicated directly through its aesthetic.

6.1   6.2   6.3   6.4   6.5

6.3
Designing
sustainable
lifestyles

126 / 127

Sustainable lifestyles

A key lesson from BedZED is the importance of considering not just the design of the buildings in which people live, but also how to design communities to help residents live sustainable lifestyles. This is still not appreciated widely enough by architects and planners, even though it is a more cost-effective way of reducing environmental impacts than solutions based primarily on infrastructure.

BioRegional has found that it is important to make it easy and convenient for people to take sustainable actions, and difficult for them to take unsustainable ones. Their monitoring of BedZED has consistently demonstrated that sustainable lifestyles account for around half of the ecological savings at BedZED. Putting these sustainable lifestyle-enabling features in place when the community was first built was key to their success.

BedZED residents consistently report that they like its strong sense of community; on average they know 20 of their neighbours, compared to the local average of eight. It is generally accepted that people who are socially engaged in this way are more likely to be happier and healthier.

BedZED represents a prototype, in which many sustainable building technologies are combined and tested in a real-life experiment in sustainable living. Ongoing assessment of its successes and failures is important to the development of our understanding of designing sustainable lifestyles. The lessons learnt from BedZED are now being applied in the commercial and social housing sectors in the UK.

Part III
Design for
sustainable
change

Chapter 6
Design for
sustainable
living

Case study
Green Mapping: 'think global, map local'

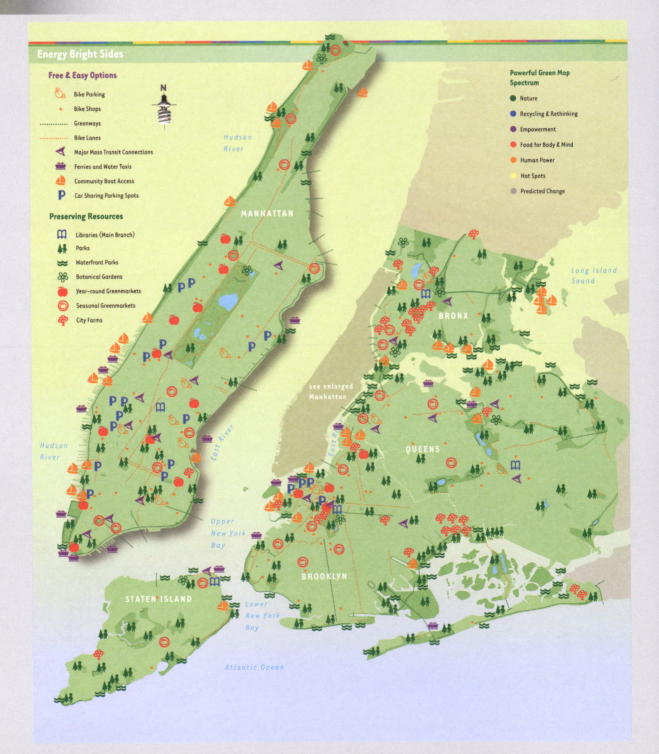

Green Maps are locally created, environmentally and socially themed maps. A Green Map plots the locations of a community's natural, cultural and sustainable resources (such as community gardens, heritage sites, recycling centres and socially conscious businesses). It combines adaptable tools and universal iconography with local knowledge and ownership, to chart options for greener living. A Green Map also brings attention to negative local features, such as toxic waste sites, which challenge community well-being. In this way, a Green Map also becomes a tool for local community and environmental activism.

Green Map System is a community of map-makers, based in New York, USA, whose goal is to help build sustainable communities through the collaborative work of searching-out and highlighting community assets via Green Maps. The goal is to encourage local involvement in cultivating more sustainable communities around the world. Wendy Brawer is Green Map System's founder and director. She has been an eco-designer, public educator and consultant since 1990. Brawer started the global Green Map System in 1995 and continues to lead its development.

According to Brawer, the function of a Green Map is simple: 'It gives you a fresh perspective on where you live; you see it from a totally new vantage point.' On a Green Map, the local environment is the foreground, not the background.

To make the process of creating Green Maps accessible to prospective map-makers from different cultures and countries, Brawer and her growing network of 'mappers' have devised a universal visual language in the form of a series of icons, for use on any Green Map. The global Green Mapping movement also shares its knowledge and experience of developing and maintaining Green Maps through training sessions, group visits, events and an active blog through a central, global website.

Green Maps are useful tools for encouraging sustainable lifestyles. A local Green Map, and the process of creating it through local participation, can have a number of positive effects:

— Raise awareness of, and expand demand for, healthier, greener lifestyle choices.

— Strengthen 'local-global' sustainability links and networks.

— Help successful green living initiatives spread to other communities.

Green Mapping is a participatory process. A Green Map is created *by*, not *for*, a community. To aid this process even further a participatory mapmaking website, the Open Green Map, has been created at www.opengreenmap. org. This is an interactive online space for sharing insights relating to local features and sites about sustainable and unsustainable living. Based on open-source and mapping technologies like Google Map, *Open Green Map* can be explored and customized online using any internet-enabled device. A Green Map iPhone app also incorporates videos, photos, blogs and digital social networking tools, so that you can use and add to a local Green Map wherever you are.

The Green Map of NYC
(left)
Wendy Brawer created the first Green Map of her native New York City in 1992. The version shown here can be easily downloaded and printed onto one letter-sized piece of paper. Visit www.opengreenmap.org/nyc for the interactive version of this map.

Part III
Design for
sustainable
change

Chapter 6
Design for
sustainable
living

Scenarios for sustainable living

It is widely recognized that our behaviours need to profoundly change, especially in the developed world, if we are to move towards more sustainable, one-planet living. How we might get there is, if we are truthful, at present rather vague. Ezio Manzini, a leading thinker in this area, suggests that this transition will occur through a shared 'social learning process through which, among mistakes and contradictions, we will all learn to live differently'.[2] This means we will have to learn to live better, but consume less, and 'regenerate our physical and social environment in an ever more closely and extensively interconnected world'.

To enable this social learning, we need to envision new possible futures at the everyday level, not just through large-scale urban planning. This approach is scenario-based, and focused on pragmatic small-scale proposals for more sustainable lifestyles. We need to learn how to generate clear, reasoned visions for improving our current lifestyles. These visions should be feasible and stimulate productive conversation between all of those involved. A process of dialogue and collaboration is paramount if we are to generate useful shared ideas about which directions to take towards a more sustainable way of living. The small-scale scenarios we create in this way may still be radical and involve a new set of social relations between members of a community. The role of the individual may be redefined in pursuit of a more sustainable collective future.

Developing scenarios for sustainable living means asking questions such as: 'what could life be like in a sustainable society?', and 'what features define any sustainable society we can imagine today?' We must focus on new 'living strategies' that result from social- and systems-innovation, rather than technological innovation. These non-technological forms of innovation need to be at the heart of our emergent new visions of how we might begin to steer our lives in a new direction. These scenarios are not, then, necessarily about envisioning a shiny new 'hi-tech' future; they are attempts to steer us towards promising signals of more sustainable living.

"If we do not change our direction, we are likely to end up where we are headed."

Chinese proverb

[2] Manzini & Jegou (2003:1)

Design-orienting scenarios (DOS): structure and characteristics

Designers could be key actors in creating scenarios for sustainable living and developing their practical applications. This is a young field of study and research, and experience and methods are still being developed. Design-orienting scenarios (DOS) is one emerging process available to designers for the conceptualization and development of these kinds of sustainable solutions. The DOS process can result in a variety of comparable visions, with clearly stated motivations and goals and demonstrated by tangible and potentially feasible proposals.

1 DOS structure

Vision
The vision for a scenario asks the basic question, 'what would the world be like if …?' It imagines a context or setting for our lives and how this might appear in the form of behaviours and proposals (in design terms – products, communications and services).

Proposal
The proposal gives concrete form to the outline vision, transforming it into a real scenario. It addresses the question, 'what has to be done to implement the vision?' It presents tangible and comprehensible sets of products and services, which are coherent with the vision and, crucially, feasible.

Motivation
Motivation gives meaning and legitimacy to the scenario. It answers the question, 'why is this scenario relevant …?' This is the most rational and technical aspect of the scenario-building process, and is composed of general and specific goals (and an assessment of their delivery).

2 DOS characteristics

Plurality
A design-orienting scenario identifies alternative solutions and/or contexts, which are evaluated in terms of their economic, social and environmental implications.

Feasibility/acceptability
A DOS is based on existing technological and/or socio-economic opportunities.

Micro-scale
A DOS relates to the scale of our lives, i.e. to the physical and socio-cultural spaces in which our individual and collective actions take place.

Visual expression
A DOS presents its imagined contexts and proposals visually, allowing us to see what they could be like.

Participation
A DOS enables the collaboration of different actors in realizing a common vision, acting as a catalyst to network and partnership building.[3]

[3] Manzini (2001)

Part III
Design for
sustainable
change

Chapter 6
Design for
sustainable
living

Interview
Ezio Manzini

Ezio Manzini
Professor of Industrial Design, Director
of the Research Unit – Design and
Innovation for Sustainability, at
Politecnico di Milano, Italy.

The Ideas Sharing Stall
(above and right)
The Feeding Milan project has
developed a tool called the Ideas
Sharing Stall for farmers' markets. The
aim is to open up discussion amongst
Milan city dwellers and designers
regarding the development of new
service concepts such as the Farmers'
Food Box. The stall actively involves
consumers and producers in the project
by using co-design tools as well as
communicating the project's initiatives.

What are the vision and key objectives of the Design for Social Innovation and Sustainability (DESIS) Network?

Before answering this question, a premise is needed. In the last decades we have been witnessing a growing wave of social innovation. Many institutions, enterprises, non-profit organizations – but also and most of all, individual citizens and their associations – have been able to move outside our mainstream models of living, to invent new and more sustainable ones. Of course, given its nature, this kind of innovation cannot be planned. But it can be made more probable, by creating favourable environments and empowering creative people with the products and services they need to support them in this endeavour.

And here, of course, is where design can play a meaningful role. Within this framework, DESIS is a network of organizations – schools of design, associations, institutions, companies – interested in promoting and supporting this new possible role for design. The specific aim of DESIS is to support social innovation worldwide, by using design skills to give promising cases more visibility, to make them more effective, and to allow them to be applied and replicated elsewhere. We also want to help companies and institutions to understand the potential of social innovation for developing services, products and new business ideas.

How did you come to focus on design for social innovation and sustainability?

For me and my colleagues, interest in design for social innovation and sustainability comes from the convergence of two areas: design for sustainability, and design and diffuse creativity. In 2004, these two areas came together in a European research project, Emerging User Demands for sustainable solutions (EMUDE), in which we focused on groups of collaborative people who were inventing and realizing sustainable ways of living. We have since observed similar work all around the world: Brazil, India, China, South Africa, Colombia, USA, Australia and the Middle East. Through the DESIS Network, we now partner with other organizations promoting social innovation.

Do you have any insights you can share regarding the designer as an actor in enabling sustainable lifestyles?

Before reinventing the wheel, look attentively at what is already happening around you. Amid the complexity of our contemporary society, it is possible to recognize creative groups of people who are inventing solutions to current problems that are, at the same time, also meaningful steps towards a sustainable way of living. Looking at these cases, we can observe that these original prototypes become more robust and widespread when they are empowered by specific sets of products and services. That is, when appropriate enabling solutions had been developed. And this, of course, is what designers can help to do.

Does this differ from country to country?

Of course, enabling solutions are necessarily very locale-specific; none should be considered as a standardized solution, to simply be replicated elsewhere. Nevertheless, there are some service ideas, supporting dedicated products and specific design knowledge, that can become building blocks to be used in different contexts to realize (most often through co-design) appropriate localized solutions.

What advice would you give to designers wanting to get involved in sustainable lifestyle projects?

Considering the scale and complexity of the challenges we face, the best approach is to search for solutions that best use existing resources (creativity, skills, entrepreneurship) wherever they might be. From research centres and universities to professional agencies; from student classes to active groups of creative people. Professional designers have to be able to operate in these new design networks. It will not be easy, but it is a fascinating challenge!

Part III
Design for
sustainable
change

Chapter 6
Design for
sustainable
living

6.4 Designing sustainable cities

According to the United Nations, over half the world's population now live in cities.[4] Migration to urban areas is a growing trend, especially in the non-Western developing world. We therefore need to consider the idea of the sustainable city and the extent to which urban living can also be sustainable living.

We might intuitively associate sustainable lifestyles more with the countryside than the city. Cities often have very visible environmental and social problems such as air pollution, traffic congestion and lack of wildlife habitat. Yet the high density of population in urban areas can actually allow for more environmentally efficient lifestyles, in terms of consumption of resources, shared access to facilities and reduced transportation needs. It may seem counter-intuitive, but cities can be more sustainable than the countryside. The idea of the sustainable city is therefore not necessarily a contradiction in terms.

Living in a city can sometimes be more sustainable than living in the countryside. This is not to say that all cities are currently sustainable; far from it. Yet there are cities around the world that are demonstrating a strong commitment to supporting sustainable lifestyles for their inhabitants. Even the most polluted city may have some successful examples of low-impact living and features that contribute positively to its residents' well-being.

Historic cities such as London have evolved over long periods of time. Other cities have grown more rapidly, or may even have been largely built as a single project, perhaps responding to rapid immigration from surrounding rural areas. We might then ask, to what extent do sustainable cities evolve? Can we set out to design a sustainable city?

[4] United Nations Population Fund *State of World Population 2007: Unleashing the potential of urban growth* (2007:1).

Case study
The city of Freiburg, Germany

Freiburg is a city of a quarter of a million inhabitants in southern Germany. It has been known since the 1960s as a self-styled green city, with non-conformist politics and a high quality of life. Freiburg has a climate protection action plan and low-carbon energy policy at city level. The city authorities have also placed great emphasis on sustainable transport and mobility, encouraging pedestrian, bicycle and public transport.

Freiburg demonstrates holistic and integrated urban planning, in pursuit of supporting sustainable lifestyles for its inhabitants. The city's spatial development plan focuses on limiting expansion of city limits and making efficient use of all existing land use. Services are decentralized, as part of a vision of being a city of short distances. New residential neighbourhoods have been created that are car-free and based around the pedestrian, and which embody high standards of passive house design requiring little heating or ventilation.

Freiburg is located in the sunniest and warmest part of Germany, giving it a clear advantage in terms of renewable energy generation. Yet its success as a pioneering sustainable city cannot be put down to that fact alone. Freiburg's success is also due in large part to city politics of cooperation and participation.

There is consensus on the importance of sustainability across all political parties in the city. Crucially, Freiburg's citizens are directly involved in the governance of the city, as shareholders in local renewable power stations, through direct participation in the spatial development plan and municipal budget and as technical experts on specialist committees. Freiburg's status as a green city is therefore largely based on the active involvement of its inhabitants in determining what kind of city they want to live in.

Freiburg represents an example of urban planning and design in which more sustainable lifestyles and behaviours are made easier to achieve. Freiburg has, perhaps more than any other modern city, been designed to be a sustainable city. Its current form represents the culmination of 40 years of radical and engaged local politics, in which a vision has been worked towards via consensus.

But, if green living is effectively made compulsory, should we be uneasy at the degree of social control that this might suggest? Might there be a risk of a backlash against these enforced lifestyle decisions? Not if the consensual politics demonstrated so far in Freiburg continues.

Freiburg, self-styled green city
(left)
Freiburg demonstrates holistic and integrated urban planning, which supports more sustainable lifestyles for its inhabitants. A number of new residential neighbourhoods have been created that are car-free and based around the pedestrian. An efficient public transportation system is key to their success.

Part III
Design for
sustainable
change

Chapter 6
Design for
sustainable
living

Case study
Transition Towns

The Transition Movement considers the sustainability challenges of the near future as opportunities to rethink the way we organize our local communities. The movement is concerned with how we can successfully negotiate the transition from an oil-dependent economy to a post-oil economy. It seeks to examine, at a local level, how threats arising from climate change and peak oil can be addressed by building local communities that are more interconnected, resilient and self-reliant.[5] A key part of the transition approach is an emphasis on localization – cutting transport miles by supplying needs locally and building community connections so that people get to know each other and become more able to work together to imagine and create a low-carbon way of living. There are transition initiatives around the world.

Transition Town Brixton

A Transition Town is a community-initiated project that rises to the transition challenge in a particular place. Most early Transition Towns in the UK have been in affluent rural locations. Transition Town Brixton in South London is the highest profile project in an urban setting. It is also, perhaps, the most interesting of these projects because of Brixton's cultural diversity. Much of the area's population comes from recent immigration and is ethnically non-white, and Brixton has a recent history of politically and racially motivated unrest and violence, including the Brixton riot of 1981. The area is also often associated with political radicalism and activism. This potentially makes Transition Town Brixton a more challenging project than its UK forebears.

The Brixton Pound
(right)
The B£ one pound note features Olive Morris, a radical political activist and community organizer who established the Brixton Black Women's Group and played a pivotal role in the squatters' rights campaigns of the 1970s. Will the Brixton Pound be a success? Can it live up to the rhetoric of the Transition Town Brixton project? That all depends on how seriously all of the local communities, from all cultures, get involved.

6.1   6.2   6.3   6.4   6.5

6.4
Designing
sustainable
cities

136 / 137

The mission of Transition Town Brixton is:

— To spread awareness of peak oil and climate change.

— To motivate a significant number of people to engage in change.

— To record actions and show the benefits of carbon-reducing measures.

— To envision a good low-energy future for Brixton and plan how to get there.

— To create the Brixton Energy Descent Action Plan.

— To put the plan into action and monitor progress, modifying as necessary.

Money that sticks to Brixton

The introduction of a local currency is a common indicator of the maturity of a particular Transition Town initiative. The Brixton Pound (B£) is the local currency introduced to Brixton. You exchange a pound sterling for a B£ one pound note, which can then only be spent with local independent businesses. Switching to the local currency in this way encourages shoppers to support local business rather than chain stores and also encourages those local businesses to source their goods and supplies from other local traders.

The B£ cannot be banked as it has no legal status and so it stays in circulation within Brixton. Customers benefit from special offers at many of the participating shops, cafes and bars, while the businesses benefit from free promotion through the B£ website, leaflets, media and so on.

The role of design?

Transition Town Brixton is not itself a design-led initiative. Many of the people involved are, however, designers by background, and many of the projects within Transition Town Brixton are design-led; for example, promoting local waste reduction, reuse and recycling through developing skills of remaking and repair. The initiative creates a context for design interventions that otherwise would not exist.

Part III
Design for
sustainable
change

Chapter 6
Design for
sustainable
living

6.5
Designing sustainable regions

Sustainability requires seeing the world as a system in which everything is connected. This applies to the things that go to make up our everyday lives, such as transportation, food and eating, spending time with family and achieving a sense of community. There are opportunities for intervening to improve the sustainability of our lifestyles at many different points. Opportunities for new ways of living exist at a number of different levels, including that of the geographic region.

Around the world, local and regional government departments are increasingly required to contribute to:
— natural resource protection
— encouragement and support of sustainable consumption and production
— mitigation of climate change
— the creation of sustainable communities.

A sustainable region is resilient, healthy, productive, socially just and lives within its environmental limits. The goal of regional and local governments, and other social innovation organizations working towards the creation of a sustainable region, is to integrate economic, social and environmental values.

This applies at the scale of major infrastructural projects — like a region's transportation system — but also to the simple activities that we perform on a daily basis. A progressive approach is to determine which activities we already perform relatively sustainably, and focus on expanding these, while at the same time finding ways to make other activities more sustainable. Design and designers can contribute to this project.

**South West of England:
vision for a sustainable region**

A growing number of regional and local governments are taking a long-term, people-focused approach to developing sustainable regions. This kind of approach is not necessarily about infrastructure. Sustainability South West, an independent body for sustainable development in the South West of England, identifies a number of key themes:

— Only use our fair share of the planet's natural resources by consuming less and using our existing resources more efficiently.

— Meet everyone's basic need for healthy food, clean water, decent housing and learning.

— Develop a thriving one planet/ low-carbon regional economy that strengthens local economies (for example, by significantly increasing the proportion of locally sourced products and services and ensuring that goods sourced from beyond the region are ethically and environmentally sound).

— Enhance the distinctiveness and diversity of the region's natural environment and biodiversity along with its built environment, heritage and cultural assets.

— Ensure access to goods, services, jobs, learning and leisure in low carbon ways.

— Meet the majority of our energy needs through local renewable energy generation.

— Fairly value everyone's contribution to society, provide satisfying work opportunities matched to local workforce needs and support a healthy work-life balance.

— Provide access for all to learning, leisure and cultural activities.

— Facilitate healthy lifestyles and caring communities to prevent poor health.

— Help people to be and feel safe from crime or persecution.

— Help everyone to learn why and how to live sustainably.

— Involve everyone in public decisions and the sustainability challenge.

— Successfully adapt to unavoidable climate change.

Part III
Design for
sustainable
change

Chapter 6
Design for
sustainable
living

Case study
Designs of the Time (Dott 07)

Designs of the Time (Dott 07)
(right)
Through Dott 07, the Design and
Sexual Health (DaSH) project used
design interventions to make sexual
health services easier to access and
use, producing a blueprint taken up by
Primary Healthcare Trusts.

Designs of the Time (Dott) is an initiative developed by the UK Design Council and its partners. In 2007, Dott 07 was the first in an intended 10-year programme of events that will take place in a series of specific regions across the UK. The second Dott initiative took place in Cornwall, England throughout 2010.

Dott 07 was the umbrella identity for a year of community projects, events and exhibitions, based in the north-east region of England, which explored what life in a sustainable region could be like, and how design could help us get there. Dott 07 was funded by the Design Council and the North East Regional Development Agency. Dott 07 represented a large-scale exploration of how social and environmental problems could be addressed by blending social innovation and design thinking with the insights and knowledge of local people. It took a deliberate interest in encouraging and supporting grass-roots innovation, rather than imported solutions.

The goal of the Dott initiative is to mobilize people around a public services and sustainability agenda, by starting with existing grass-roots activity and then creating frameworks that enable these activities to develop. Dott seeks to put people at the centre of the redesign of public services, and so the role of the designer in Dott 07 was to facilitate collaborative activity among larger groups of people, rather than to dream up new blue-sky solutions. In Dott 07's public design commissions, the local public was the client and also the co-designer. Problems from rural transport to sustainable food production were collaboratively identified, defined, and worked through to find and prototype solutions.

Dott's overall vision is that design can generate grass-roots innovation that ultimately leads to new and better services. Projects in Dott 07 aimed to improve five aspects of daily life in the region: movement, health, food, school and energy.

The Low Carb Lane project, for example, led to an innovative financial package to help low-income households cut their carbon emissions, and the concept is now being implemented with regional funding.

Dott 07, through its wide range of projects, provided a context for the emergence of innovative new modes of design practice in the UK. A cohort of new designers have used their involvement in Dott as a springboard for defining innovative new roles for themselves, working in new contexts and adding value not just to business, but also to the public sector and to society as a whole.

Seven roles of the designer in Dott 07

Lauren Tan undertook a major research project into the role of design and designers in the Dott 07 initiative. She identified a set of roles adopted by designers through their involvement in the project:

1 **Co-creator**
Co-designing with people, rather than for them.

2 **Communicator**
Using communication devices to enable communities to have conversations around issues.

3 **Strategist**
Devising plans of creative action to engage communities in tackling issues.

4 **Capability builder**
Building design-led skills among people to address challenges themselves.

5 **Entrepreneur**
Creating powerful ideas to improve people's lives and spreading them society-wide.

6 **Researcher**
Using design research to bring people-centred perspectives to product and service development.

7 **Facilitator**
Bringing together communities using design-led tools to act upon issues.

Chapter 7
Design for development

7.0

The sustainability agenda is closely linked to the development agenda. Design for sustainability, as it derives from the concept of sustainable development, must simultaneously address ecological health and human development, the two are inextricably connected on both a local and global scale. Development is the term used to describe the route out of poverty for those with a low quality of life. Yet it is misguided to pursue economic and material wealth without considering the potential environmental and social consequences.

Development is concerned with poverty alleviation. Sustainable development seeks to alleviate poverty but not at the expense of global ecological health and well-being. Sustainable development takes a long view of human development and recognizes that rapid short-term poverty alleviation may not necessarily be the best goal if it has harmful ecological consequences. This chapter explores a range of approaches to designing for development from around the world, all of which embody local solutions.

Part III
Design for
sustainable
change

Chapter 7
Design for
development

7.1
Designing against inequality

The predominant model for the design profession is a corporate one; most designers work for clients who are serving and responding to markets. Some designers, however, reject this model and address overtly social and environmental causes, irrespective of whether or not they relate to commercial markets. These designers may be in the minority compared to those in mainstream commercial practice, but they are demonstrating alternative new approaches and roles. An increasing number of them are responding to Victor Margolin's call to '…look at economic and social development from a global perspective, and address the gross inequalities of consumption between people in the industrialized countries and those in the developing world.'[1]

What is development?

The dominant measure of national economic output, Gross Domestic Product (GDP), has until recently often been taken as a simple proxy for quality of life and well-being. On this reckoning, a rich nation is a healthy and happy nation. As a measure of prosperity, however, GDP only considers *economic* gains and losses, expressed in monetary terms. This is clearly misleading; a country may experience a dramatic increase in GDP that may mask human rights abuses, widespread poverty and environmental degradation. Should we then call that nation developing? If we only judge by economics, then the answer may be yes – but there are clearly other factors to be considered.

[1] Margolin (1998:92)
[2] Whiteley (1993:41)
[3] Korten (1999:62)
[4] Balaram (2009:54)

More holistic measurements of national well-being have been created, such as the United Nations Human Development Index (HDI), which presents new ways of measuring development by considering indicators such as life expectancy and educational attainment, as well as financial wealth (see pages 84–85). The continuing dominance of GDP as a global proxy for levels of development, however, represents an institutionalization of economic growth as the most important indicator of well-being, despite its obvious shortcomings.

Inequality within societies

Richard Wilkinson and Kate Pickett's controversial book *The Spirit Level* examines the apparently life-diminishing results of internal inequality within societies. Their analysis of social trends in 23 economically developed countries finds that inequality of income within those societies seems to be reflected in shorter, unhealthier and unhappier lives for all members of those societies, not just the poorest. They find evidence of direct relationships between inequality and health (particularly mental health) and social problems. Hyper-consumerism, isolation, alienation, social estrangement and anxiety in all sectors of the community are apparently linked to the inequality found in economically developed nations.

This analysis suggests that a nation's economic income is not a reliable indicator of its overall well-being. Equal distribution of wealth, rather than overall wealth, creates a well society. The difference between a nation's rich and poor is more important than the difference between that nation's wealth and the wealth of other nations. If this is the case, it alters our conception of development and of how and where we might intervene as designers seeking to address societal needs. Design for development is no longer something that takes place just in the developing world; it may be needed in South London just as much as in Southern India.

Think globally, design locally

Designers seeking to address the consequences of inequality, whether in South London or Southern India, need a clear sense of what they are trying to achieve and how to go about it. Those involved in 'socially conscious design'[2] and 'people-centred development'[3] increasingly argue that this vision needs to be oriented towards small-scale initiatives that are local, cooperative and resource-efficient, but also with a global and long-term perspective. In other words, we should think globally, but design locally. We should view development not just in economic terms, but as an economic, social, cultural and political process.

This is not a new concept. In 1957, the then prime minister of India, Jawaharlal Nehru invited the eminent American designers Charles and Ray Eames to advise his government on an appropriate design strategy for the country. The prime minister was specifically interested in the issue of how to help India's vast craft sector and its small-scale industries make the necessary transition into the era of industrialization. Nehru wanted to find an appropriate Indian solution that was not simply an imitation of what was happening in the already industrialized nations. In the India Report (1958), the Eames' called for a design industry that respected what Indians held to be important for a good life, and which incorporated an understanding of the values and qualities that contributed to it.[4]

"Development is a comprehensive economic, social, cultural and political process, which aims at the constant improvement of the well-being of the entire population and of all individuals on the basis of their active, free and meaningful participation in development and in the fair distribution of benefits resulting therefrom."

United Nations General Assembly
Declaration on the Right to Development (1986)

Part III
Design for
sustainable
change

Chapter 7
Design for
development

7.2
Designing for needs, not wants

Maslow's hierarchy of needs
(right)
The psychologist Abraham Maslow
devised his famous hierarchy as a
way of attempting to understand
what motivates people in their actions
and goals. The hierarchy is based
on the idea of pre-potency, whereby
a particular need only arises for an
individual when the needs below it
have been satisfied. The hierarchy
is a model, and so not an absolutely
accurate guide to every human action.
It does, however, help us to understand
the different types of human need for
which we might be designing, and that
some needs (such as our physiological
need for food and water) are more
fundamental to existence than others.[6]

[5] Max-Neef (1991)
[6] Maslow (1943)
[7] The World Bank (2008)

Transcendence

Self-actualization

Aesthetic needs

Need to know and understand

Esteem needs

Belongingness and love needs

Safety needs

Physiological needs

Needs versus wants

Designers may not want to design only for the privileged few. They may want to direct their expertise towards more meaningful challenges, and to design for real *needs*, rather than artificially created *wants*. But what are these real or true needs? In his book *Design for the Real World*, the designer Victor Papanek uses Abraham Maslow's famous hierarchy of needs to identify projects that designers should be working on. For Papanek, designers have a moral responsibility to design for people whose basic needs are not being met.

More recently, the Chilean economist Manfred Max-Neef has proposed the concept of Human Scale Development, based on the satisfaction of the following 'fundamental' human needs:
— Subsistence
— Protection
— Affection
— Understanding
— Participation
— Leisure
— Creation
— Identity
— Freedom [5]

These needs are fixed and universal to all people in all times. They are also finite and satisfiable, in contrast to wants, which are infinite and insatiable. These needs should also be distinguished from the satisfiers by which they are met. Owning a car can help us to satisfy our need for leisure, but we shouldn't view owning a car as a need in itself; it is a means to an end. Max-Neef sees no hierarchy of needs, apart from the basic needs for survival. The fundamental needs are instead all interrelated and interactive.

Designers seeking to respond to needs rather than wants must therefore think carefully about how they make this distinction, and recognize that really wanting something is not always the same as truly needing it. Design outcomes are also instrumental: they are means to ends, rather than ends in themselves. The fundamental question for a designer therefore becomes, 'What need am I addressing through my design?'

Poverty alleviation

Globally, significant numbers of people every day go hungry, do not have access to clean water and live in temporary shelter. The World Bank's 2008 Poverty Data [7] shows that there are 1.4 billion people living in extreme poverty, on less than $1.25 a day. This includes 42 per cent of the people living in developing countries. Over the last 15 years, global poverty has fallen by an average of one per cent per year, but large differences in income remain between regions, across countries in the same region, and within countries. There are more extremely poor people and poverty is reaching farther into middle-income countries.

In response, there is growing interest in employing design and design thinking to improve the lives of those living in poverty. Social and product innovations are created not to maximize profits, but to address true needs, and alleviate poverty and environmental degradation. These design interventions are intended to help economically poor and disadvantaged people in developed and developing countries alike.

"Much recent design has satisfied only evanescent *wants and desires*, while the *genuine needs* of man have often been neglected by the designer."

Victor Papanek
Design for the Real World (1984:15)

Part III
Design for
sustainable
change

Chapter 7
Design for
development

7.3
Approaches
to designing for
development

Victor Papanek's hierarchy of ways in which designers can usefully intervene in 'under-developed and emergent nations'

The higher up Papanek's hierarchy a designer can work the better (in other words, option 1 is the ideal). Design for development is above all about empowering people. Embedding design capability in the people we are seeking to support is the most powerful intervention we can make as designers. This framework does not, however, reflect more recent emphasis on *participatory* approaches to design for development. Many recent examples focus on designing *with*, rather than designing *for*, people in need.

1 Train designers to train more designers; in, for example, Tanzania.

2 Train designers; in Tanzania.

3 Design for people in Tanzania; in Tanzania.

4 Design for people in Tanzania; from London.[8]

[8] Papanek (1971, 1984:84)

How can a designer from an industrialized country usefully intervene in a developing world context? We might first ask the broader question, how can *any* designer usefully intervene in a context unknown to them and which is characterized by poverty, or where basic needs are not being met? The second question acknowledges that design for development may not always involve a designer from the rich global North intervening in the poor global South, with all the potential post-colonial and cultural sensitivities that this might bring. That design for development *is* usually presented as acting in one direction does not mean that it always needs to be so.

This section presents a number of examples of how design is being used effectively and how designers are working around the world with communities in need of development. These examples do not all fit a conventional design for the 'third world' model. To consider design for development as being akin to design for the Third World risks reinforcing the distinctions between different parts of the world – many designers are trying to challenge these negative distinctions.

In any situation in which a designer intervenes, the designer should strive to have a long-lasting influence that does not end when they move on. They should seek to embed design awareness, capabilities and skills with the people they work with. Those people will then be able to continue to exploit design for their own benefit, without relying on the continued involvement of an outside agency. In this way, design can aid self-sufficiency and empower people in developing parts of the world to devise their own solutions to their own challenges.

A key challenge for designers seeking to work on design for development projects is finding or creating appropriate opportunities. Should every designer donate ten per cent of their professional time to development projects, as altruistic or pro bono work? Should designers seek to incorporate development principles into the work they do already? Should design for development be pursued outside, or within, the market-driven consumerist economic system? The examples presented here provide different responses to these questions.

Charity or enterprise?

Most of the world's designers spend most of their time designing for the world's richest ten per cent of the world's population. There is clearly huge scope for these designers to address the real problems faced daily by the other 90 per cent: the world's poor. Initiatives to support these designers do exist, and are driven and funded not just by governmental and non-governmental organizations, but also by social enterprises and for-profit businesses. This enterprise approach to poverty relief is based on the belief that the more conventional approach, charity, is expensive and simply creates dependency.

Critics of the enterprise model in turn fear that low-cost innovations targeted at developing countries are often created in high-tech, glamorous design studios in major cities, rather than being developed at a local level with their intended users. The inherent danger is that such designs may not only be unsuccessful in meeting the needs of their intended users, but they may also be perceived as patronizing. This may be felt particularly strongly by innovators in those developing countries, who may be limited in their capacity to develop and distribute their own designs because of a lack of financial capital.

"Designers are the key to showing how to mobilize cutting-edge technologies, new materials, and new approaches to older materials and technologies, in order to solve problems such as clean water… low-cost housing, internet connectivity for the poor, and much more... Typically, path-breaking approaches can be found at low cost. Once these are proved, then they can be taken to scale through a combination of market incentives, development assistance and large-scale philanthropic efforts."

Jeffrey Sachs
Designing An End to Poverty
www.design21sdn.com/feature/930

Part III
Design for
sustainable
change

Chapter 7
Design for
development

Local design for local needs

There are examples of small enterprises in countries such as South Africa and India, innovating products that more successfully meet the needs of the poor in those countries. This is a relatively new way of thinking about enterprise-based poverty alleviation, and one which raises an additional question of finance. How can these local enterprises sell to those in need what they need now, rather than having to wait until their customers have saved the money to buy what others already have? There is a danger that over-zealous attempts to market and sell affordable products to the poor can come at the expense of quality. Cheap, less effective products are no good to anyone. The key to addressing poverty through selling locally produced products is to focus on how the poor can become investors or even co-innovators, rather than simply consumers. Involving the people that a design project is intended to benefit is vitally important.

Understanding the local conditions, needs and economic realities of the identified people is critical to the success and sustainability of any project, be it charitable or entrepreneurial. An outside agency, therefore, needs trusted field partners to help it to understand local users and their environment, to enable it to successfully design for their needs.

Designs for the poor are not however a cure-all. Small-scale technology and design interventions can only go so far to resolve poverty and protect environmental conditions. Large-scale change requires wider infrastructural and political intervention.

Designers and the craft sector in developing countries

Any consideration of design for development must also consider the role of craft. Crafts produce handmade products, which are often both functional and deeply culturally rooted. In many developing nations, handcraft production is a major mode of employment and can constitute a significant part of the export economy.

People in developing countries who get their income from making artefacts for sale are generally called artisans or crafters, rather than designers. According to the United Nation's *Creative Economy Report 2008*, crafts are the only creative industry in which developing countries have a leading position in the global market [9].

How can designers assist these artisans, while respecting and preserving local resources, rich cultural traditions and indigenous designs and products? The non-profit organization Aid to Artisans (ATA) believes that traditional artisanry survives only when traditional artisans thrive economically. To support this, ATA hire American and European designers who have knowledge of the industries and markets for home décor, gifts and fashion accessories. Through product development collaborations, ATA aims to blend global market needs with traditional craft techniques and indigenous motifs. The goal is to inspire new possibilities for creative artisanry, which add value to existing handmade traditions.

The $25 treadle pump
(left)
One approach to enterprise-led poverty relief is to deliver low-cost, locally made engineering solutions to micro-businesses in the developing world. The non-profit organization D-Rev-developed $25 (£16) treadle pump is a simple, foot-powered irrigation system. Irrigation allows farmers to grow a wide range of crops out of season. When they can diversify, they are no longer subsistence farmers; becoming economically empowered business people.

9 Hnatow (2009:1)

Through an innovative application of design, local craft can become more than a subsistence activity and develop into a satisfying and profitable global business.

The ATA design consultants also develop creative solutions to challenges such as raw material preparation, appropriate technology, environmentally sound production methods and quality control. Producing a saleable product is simply the first step. The ultimate goal is a product that can be reproduced repeatedly with consistent quality, at affordable cost, in an environmentally considered way and without compromising the health and well-being of the artisans. ATA also recommend that their design consultants should mentor local artisans both in person and long distance, to provide an ongoing and direct market perspective. When a design consultant works side by side with a local artisan, the artisan is exposed to international market trends that will hopefully inspire new marketable products.

Empowering women

Designers supporting artisans is one model for sustainable development, beyond a focus on industrial development. By creating productive employment opportunities, crafts can enhance more equitable income distribution. This is extremely important for people living in poverty, for women and for disabled people and for other marginalized groups in developing countries.

A great deal more women than men are involved in craft production in developing countries. Craft is therefore often of greatest importance, and potentially greatest benefit, to women in these countries. Craft can be a significant driver of female empowerment in parts of the world that are dominated by patriarchal social structures. Micro-credit schemes, through which small, unsecured cash loans are made to the rural poor in developing countries, are aimed overwhelmingly at women.

Ownership of the means of production, and the finance to make it happen, can raise women in particular out of poverty and dependence across the developing world.

The influence of new markets

Craft production is not, however, driven solely by economic need. Craft is also fundamentally about generating visual and material representations of the maker's culture and heritage. This can raise some interesting questions, such as 'to what extent does a designer involved in craft for development initiatives need to preserve or adapt traditional craft skills?' Does the designer need to keep alive, or challenge, embedded and long-standing cultural practices? Traditional styles and aesthetics may be challenged by the demands of new consumers in new markets.

Crafters in developing nations may be encouraged to produce artefacts for export, as these markets may be more lucrative. This may, however, require traditional crafts to be adapted to Western tastes and expectations. Notions of authenticity, real or invented, may affect what is produced. Does it matter if a traditional piece of decorated earthenware is made smaller to fit in the overhead locker of an aeroplane? Is tradition more or less important than saleability? These are conundrums faced by organizations and those involved in seeking to use craft as a vehicle for economic empowerment.

"Crafts reduce migration to cities, significantly helping women through increased income and status. Crafts assure women of cash over which they have control, expanding their economic choices, providing higher self-esteem and further developing their skills… Extended to nations, the trade in crafts increases the influx of foreign exchange… Crafts help preserve cultural identity by reconciling their unique and artistic as well as their social and economic value."

Caroline Ramsay Merriam
Characteristics of World Trade in Crafts,
(2000:1)

Part III
Design for
sustainable
change

Chapter 7
Design for
development

Case study
Industree Crafts Foundation

There are many examples of championed craft for development projects in developing countries. These are generally relatively small-scale, localized operations, initiated and managed by passionate individuals driven by a desire to improve the lot of craft-producing artisans in a particular area. An alternative model is that of Industree Crafts, a hybrid social enterprise comprised of for-profit and non-profit entities, based in Bangalore, India.

There are an estimated 40 million rural artisans in India today.[10] While global demand for Indian artisan products is growing, both in India and abroad, rural artisans largely remain poor. At the same time, India has recently emerged as a global economic force with a growing middle class. There is a new generation of socially responsible consumers in India's urban centres, rooted in their ethnicity yet also aspiring to modernity. Industree Crafts is aiming to make economic links between rural unemployment, traditional artisan craft and India's growing internal consumer market.

Industree Crafts helps individual artisans to collectivize into self-governed producer groups, which then receive capacity-building support, technical assistance and entrepreneurial training. Each producer group effectively functions as a mini-enterprise, producing and trading its goods with Industree and other buyers. Industree's mission is to improve the livelihoods of rural artisans by marketing their products to urban markets, both in India and abroad.

Product designers Neelam Chhiber and Poonam Bir Kasturi, and social investor Gita Ram, started Industree Crafts in 1994. Their first store opened in 1996, and the company began exporting products to America and Europe in 1998. It transpired that Industree could not function successfully as a social enterprise while also operating as a for-profit organization. The additional costs of reaching, engaging and training rural artisans were too substantial to support a strictly for-profit model. Indian government funding was available to build rural capacity but not granted to for-profit companies. And so, Industree Crafts Foundation (ICF) was established in 2000.

Kishore Biyani, founder of India's retail giant Future Group, became ICF's major investor. There was an advantage in working with a successful multi-brand retailer and the potential of reaching the growing Indian green consumer. The first Mother Earth retail store opened in Bangalore in April 2009. The ambition of ICF is to open 40 stores all over India in the next five years. Mother Earth aims to build a green brand image, carrying primarily organic and natural products ranging from textiles and home décor to clothing, food and gifts.

The ICF vision is on an increasingly large scale, but the Foundation intends to continue sourcing directly from producers whenever possible, and giving as much of its financial margin as possible to the rural artisans on whom the project depends. ICF is in its early stages; but it seems genuine in its aim to balance a for-profit business approach with its sustainable social-enterprise mission.

[10] Miller, Dawans and Alter (2009:2)

7.1   7.2   7.3
**Approaches
to designing for
development**

152 / 153

Industree Crafts
(above and left)
Industree sources the textiles, gifts and
furniture for sale in its Mother Earth–
branded retail shops domestically in
India.

Part III
Design for
sustainable
change

Chapter 7
Design for
development

Case study
Design for
the Other 90%
exhibition

Design for the other 90%
(left and below)
The LifeStraw is a personal mobile
water-purification tool, designed
to turn any surface water into safe
drinking water. Waterborne diseases
are estimated to cause more than two
million deaths annually. The LifeStraw
is intended for use in Ghana, Nigeria,
Pakistan and Uganda.

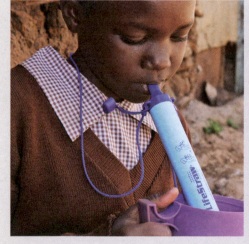

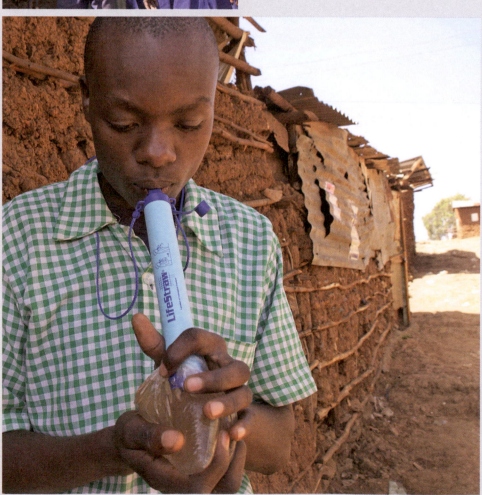

Design for the Other 90% is a touring exhibition of low-cost innovations, created by architects, designers and design teams from around the world, aimed at providing for the basic human needs of shelter, health, water, education, energy and transport. The title of the exhibition derives from the statistic that 90 per cent of the world's 6.5 billion people have little or no access to most of the products and services that many of us take for granted and consider essential. The exhibited designs range in scale from a personal water purifier to shelters for the homeless. In each case, design is used to harness often very simple technology with the goal of aiding human survival in under-developed contexts. Aesthetics are secondary in the exhibition's consideration of what qualifies as good design; function, user-centredness and affordability are key.

Many of the featured designs also aim to be produced in the place of their intended use and constructed by their users (for example, a do-it-yourself irrigation and water-storage system). Many of the products are intended for parts of the world lacking grid electricity and so must use alternative energy sources; for example, a solar home lighting system, which provides a safe alternative to dangerous lighting systems dependent on oil.

Designing from a distance?

Design for the Other 90% debuted at New York's Cooper-Hewitt, National Design Museum in 2007, and was still touring the USA in 2010; its audience is therefore resolutely Western. The exhibition showcases designs that address essential needs. Most of the featured products are, unsurprisingly, envisaged for use in developing countries. Most of the featured designers are not from the countries they are designing for (to quote the exhibition's title).

This leaves many of the exhibited design solutions open to the criticism that, while they may be well-intended, they are remote solutions created (in the words of David Stairs) by 'outsiders, who cannot begin to imagine the vicissitudes of life in such distant places'.[11] Is it inevitable that designs conceived from a developed-world mindset will fail to appreciate the 'values, perspectives and social mores' of their intended users in under-developed settings? Real-world engagement with those users is no guarantee of success in designing for them; even if a Western designer travels, he takes his Western mindset with him. Remaking the developing world in the image of the developed world, materially or culturally, is not the best approach.

"Design for the Other 90% [is] intended to draw attention to a kind of design that is not particularly attractive, often limited in function, and extremely inexpensive. It also has the inherent ability to transform and, in some cases, actually save human lives."

Barbara Bloemink
Design for the Other 90% catalogue (2007:5)

[11] Stairs (2007)

Part III
Design for
sustainable
change

Chapter 7
Design for
development

Case study
Motivation

Motivation is a design-led charity working to improve the quality of life of people with limited mobility in low-income countries around the world, including Eastern Europe. Motivation is best-known for its range of manual wheelchairs, designed to fit the needs and requirements of users in a particular place, and made using locally available materials and construction technologies. The wheelchairs are designed by a core team based in the UK, but manufactured by local people in the country in which they will be used.

There are an estimated 20 million people globally who need a wheelchair but do not have one. [12] These are often among the most disadvantaged and impoverished people in society. Poor people with disabilities are often caught in a vicious cycle of poverty and disability, each being a cause and a consequence of the other.

Motivation was co-founded by the industrial designer David Constantine, a wheelchair user himself following a spinal cord injury when he was 21 years old. Constantine is very aware of the challenges faced by wheelchair users, even in economically developed societies. The challenges faced by those in *need* of a wheelchair and living in low-income societies are even greater.

Motivation began by focusing on the provision of low-cost, appropriately designed wheelchairs for use in developing countries. A wheelchair provides someone with the means to mobility, allowing them to take an active part in their community, and opening-up employment opportunities; but this is not in itself enough. Wheelchair users still have specific physical, economic and social needs, and Motivation now also addresses these by advocating for equality of opportunity and the rights of disabled people around the world.

Motivation
(right)
There are indications that only a minority of those in need of a wheelchair have access to them, and of these very few have access to an appropriate wheelchair.[13] Eighty per cent of people with disabilities live in developing countries.[14] In response, Motivation has established Worldmade Wheelchair Services, a non-profit programme which supplies a range of appropriate wheelchairs and other mobility products across the developing world.

[12] Sheldon and Jacobs (2006)
[13] Sheldon and Jacobs (2006)
[14] United Nations. Conventions on the Rights of Persons with Disabilities (2007)

Motivation has also established Worldmade Wheelchair Services, a non-profit programme which supplies a range of appropriate wheelchairs and other mobility products, working through a network of service partners across the developing world. Worldmade is focused on establishing effective wheelchair services; it trains local organizations to carry out an assessment of a wheelchair user's needs and then prescribe, assemble and fit the most appropriate product from a supplied range. The Worldmade programme represents a scaling up of Motivation's original approach; wheelchair kits are supplied in flat-pack form and everything else is then done locally, including training in how to use the new wheelchair. Motivation's approach is focused on empowerment of the individual wheelchair user and those involved in providing the local services to support the effective use of wheelchairs in a particular place.

"We have moved on from being very technically focused, to look at the whole quality of life for people with mobility disabilities. It's about far more than just supplying a piece of equipment."

David Constantine
Third Sector (7 April 2004)

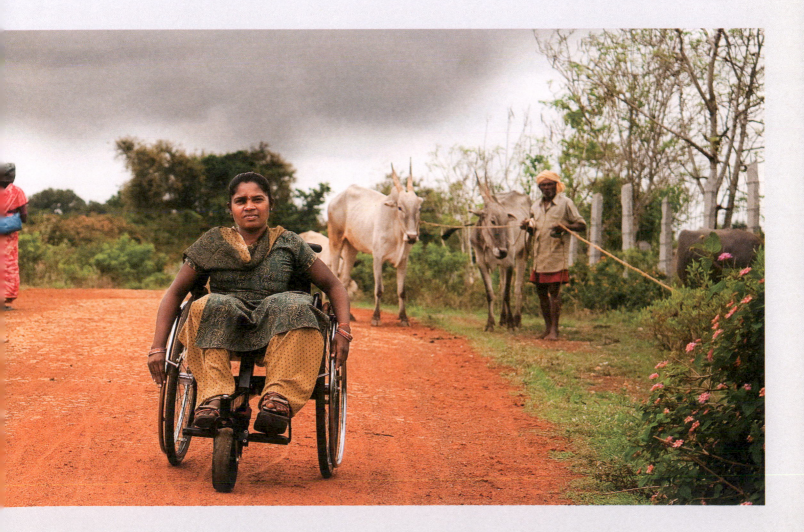

Part III
Design for
sustainable
change

Chapter 7
Design for
development

Case study
IDEO Human-Centered Design (HCD) Toolkit

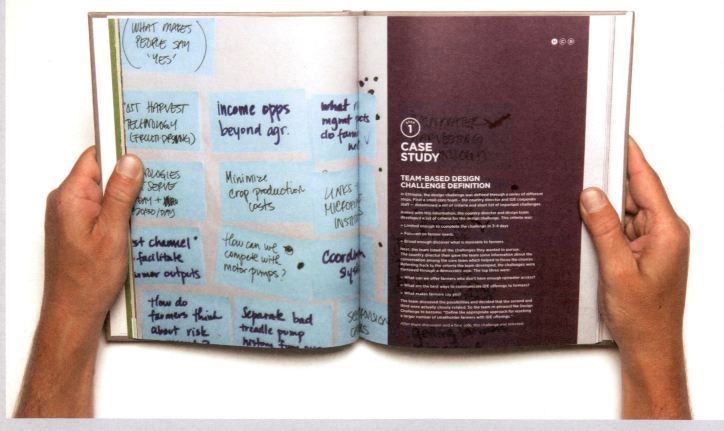

Human-Centered Design (HCD) Toolkit
(above and right)
IDEO's Toolkit adapts Human-Centered Design methodology for use by NGO staff and volunteers in developing nation and local settings. It is designed to be usable by someone with a very basic understanding of design thinking and design.

The process starts with a specific design challenge and goes through three phases: hear, create and deliver. It moves from concrete observations about people, to insights and abstract thinking to tangible solutions. Very practical advice is also given, for example on interacting with local people.

7.1   7.2   7.3
Approaches
to designing for
development

158 / 159

The Human-Centered Design (HCD) Toolkit is a free-to-download innovation guide for non-governmental organizations (NGOs) and social enterprises working with impoverished communities in Africa, Asia and Latin America, it can be accessed from www. ideo.com/work. The Toolkit contains the key elements of HCD methodology, adapted for use by NGO staff and volunteers. The HCD Toolkit helps those using it to understand people's real needs, find innovative and appropriate solutions to meet those needs and deliver financially viable and enduring outcomes. It was created by IDEO, the global innovation and design firm that has pioneered the use of human-centred design and innovation in advanced economies.

The Toolkit is essentially made up of general advice on using an HCD process (use multi-disciplinary and gender-balanced teams, dedicated spaces and finite time frames), a set of printed resources (including multiple copies of commonly used printed sheets) and guidance on their use. For the hear phase, for example, guidance is offered on 'who to talk to', 'how to gain empathy' and 'how to capture stories'. The Toolkit is designed to be flexible in use, although a number of use-scenarios are given: the week-long 'deep dive'; the several-month 'deep dive'; activating already-existing knowledge; complementing existing long-term activities. The role of the HCD 'facilitator' as the person who leads the team through the process, is key and the Toolkit contains numerous cautions for the facilitator not to exert any undue authority over the other participants.

The HCD Toolkit is intended to facilitate active participation by local people in the early problem-setting phase of the design process. It supports early field research. The Toolkit is intended to be shared with non-designers, in order to spread the influence of design thinking and increase the collective understanding of design among non-specialists. The HCD Toolkit could be used by local people, as well as NGO staff and volunteers, enabling them to design with their own community. It is not geared solely toward outsiders coming into impoverished places. The Toolkit is also open source, so it can be modified and enhanced by all its users as an aid to participatory and inclusive design processes.

Part III
Design for
sustainable
change

Chapter 7
Design for
development

Case study
The Crisis Christmas project

Crisis is the national UK charity for single homeless people. It is dedicated to ending homelessness by delivering life-changing services and campaigning for change. The Crisis Christmas project began in 1971 as a response to the plight of the homeless who might be on the streets when their usual hostels closed over the Christmas period. Crisis Christmas provides accommodation and services for the homeless community in London over the Christmas week. The event takes place in vacant buildings or in schools and colleges that would otherwise be empty over the holiday period. These centres offer support and companionship to people who are homeless or vulnerably housed, providing them with access to essential medical, counselling and advice services.

Architecture for Humanity UK

Architecture for Humanity UK (AfH UK) is the UK chapter of Architecture for Humanity. AfH UK is a charity that provides professional assistance to organizations based in the UK who need help with projects relating to the built environment. They started in 2004 as a small group of individuals who met to discuss how they could contribute their skills and expertise to help communities in need. Their vision was to promote good design, for the public benefit, in situations of social and economic deprivation, particularly in the UK. AfH UK explicitly recognizes that 'architecture for humanity' can be as needed in affluent nations like the UK as much as it is elsewhere. AfH UK is managed and delivered entirely by volunteers.

Light up my life
(left)
Various homely elements are brought into the vacant buildings to make them more welcoming. These include cut-outs of lamp and fireplace elements to create focal points in large spaces for relaxation and social interaction. These are made from chipboard sheet tessellated to minimize waste.

Crisis Christmas centres

Since 2005, Crisis and AfH UK have collaborated in designing the Crisis Christmas centres. In 2008, four residential and four day centres were established, with over 1000 guests making use of the services over the Christmas week. AfH UK produces a detailed manual for the Crisis Christmas project, setting out requirements for both successful design of the centres themselves and effective project management in terms of who does what. The group also directly provides the following services to the project:

— Developing design briefs for the centres; including careful space-planning and way-finding for different areas, interior design and furniture layout.

— Designing and constructing modules and components for the centres; including signage, lighting and festive decorations.

— Volunteer help in actually making and building the centres on site.

The Crisis Christmas project has to be delivered extremely quickly. It initially took place at different sites each year. The volunteer architects would not know the building they had to work with until a few weeks before Christmas. Transforming an unknown and uninviting space, such as a disused bullion store in South London, into a welcoming festive environment is clearly a huge challenge.

The project now often reuses the same buildings and the same design interventions each year, making the project simpler to administer and more sustainable in its reuse of donated materials and resources.

Charities using design

The Crisis Christmas project demonstrates how a charity can collaborate with a design organization to fulfil its aims. The project had existed for several years before the designers and architects became involved, and the impact of their intervention is clear to see. The use of outside design expertise by charities and non-profit organizations relates to the discussion of design activism in Chapter 3.

Projects like Crisis Christmas provide designers with opportunities to apply their unique capabilities to causes that are often simply not recognized by mainstream, commercially driven professional design practice. Charities can provide powerful vehicles for designers to directly pursue a progressive social agenda. These types of collaboration might also provide more satisfying work for the designer than is to be found in a typical commercial client-service relationship.

The Crisis Christmas project
(above and left)
Since 2005, AfH UK has collaborated in designing Crisis Christmas centres, transforming vacant and derelict buildings into welcoming and comfortable places where homeless people can come together to eat, socialize and celebrate.

Part III
Design for
sustainable
change

Chapter 7
Design for
development

Case study
Design for the First World

Design for the First World:
the rest saving the West
(below)
Design for the First World is a design
competition that reverses the usual
North-to-South direction of design
for development, and turns our
assumptions on their head. This is
'design for the other 10%'.

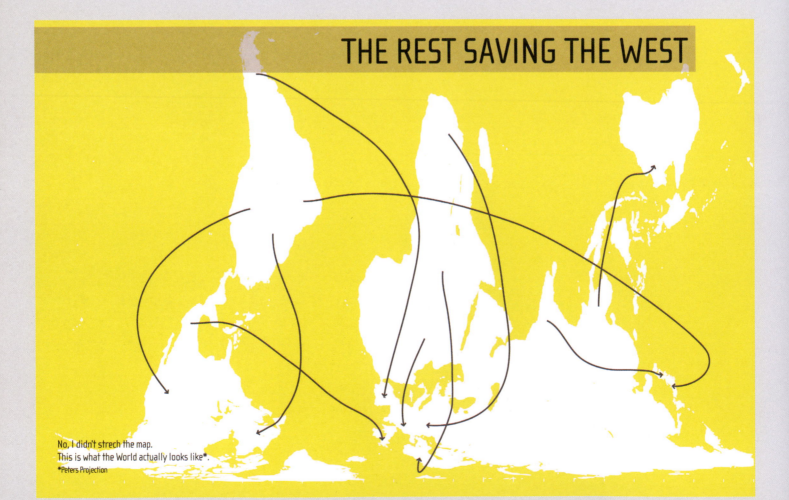

THE REST SAVING THE WEST

No, I didn't strech the map.
This is what the World actually looks like*.
*Peters Projection

7.1   7.2   7.3
Approaches
to designing for
development

162 / 163

Design For the First World is a competition open only to designers from the so-called developing world. It reverses the usual focus and direction of design for development by seeking proposals from the global South that address societal problems and challenges in the advanced economies of the global North. Obesity, consumerism, integration of immigration and ageing population are first-world issues to which third-world designers are invited to respond. Humorous and ironic designs are encouraged, but entries must propose credible solutions to identified problems. Any citizen or resident of a developing country over 13 years old can enter. The competition judges are also all from nations in the developing world.

Design For the First World is a parody of other design competitions, but it has a serious intent. It does not set out to question the need for aid in the developing world, or to mock the good intentions of designers in the developed world. Instead, it seeks to target the paternalistic and misdirected forms of intervention, which waste resources and cause more harm than good in the long run. The competition is a critique of remote or parachute designing, through which seemingly well-designed objects aimed at improving the lives of people in an undeveloped setting often overlook the real problems faced by those people, and end up as children's toys or part of the furniture. The title and concept of Design For the First World is intended to be funny, but then forces us to consider why it is funny. The competition prompts serious self-reflection on the part of designers from both the developed and developing worlds. Designing with cultural relevance is equally difficult no matter in which direction the designer is attempting to translate their experience.

Design For the First World questions the principle of 'designing for the other 90%', and the very notion of development. It poses a number of rhetorical questions; are people in developed countries happier or healthier? Do they live a better life? Do they have a better understanding of nature and live in a better equilibrium with the environment? Do they live in peace? The answer to all of which is clearly, 'no'. The competition is implicitly asking its participants, what does it mean to be a developing country, and where might development lead us?

"Our fellows in the First World often come to visit and give us their well-intentioned but often very problematic 'solutions'. We thought, why don't we pay back? Dx1W is a competition for designers, artists, scientists, makers and thinkers in developing countries to provide solutions for First World problems."

www.designforthefirstworld.com

Part III
Design for
sustainable
change

Chapter 7
Design for
development

Interview
John Ballyn

John Ballyn
Independent Design Consultant and
Contractor

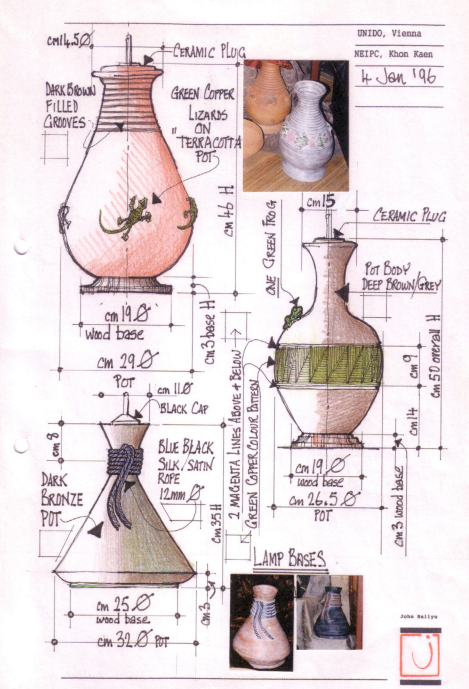

Ways of working
(above and left)
The image above is a typical design
drawing that could be made in any
situation, augmented with small photos
at a later date. The photograph of wood
carvers in Mandalay (left) shows some
of the artisans John Ballyn worked with
and the techniques they used.

How did you come to work in design for development?

My entry into development was pure serendipity. I worked for ten years within UK industrial manufacturing. Through a newspaper advert I obtained a position as head of product design at the Pakistan Design Institute in Karachi. Returning to the UK, I found any return to my previous UK design work increasingly pointless. In 1979, I was appointed as producer assistance manager at Oxfam Trading, a UK alternative trading organization. I remained there for nearly ten years, travelling extensively in Asia and Africa, living and working closely with artisan groups developing products for the makers to sell. After that I never really stopped.

Would you agree that designing for the 'other', wherever they may be, is difficult? Is it really possible to design without borders?

Regardless of nationality, most designers emerge from more developed, more sophisticated, perhaps urban and possibly better-educated backgrounds than most of the people with whom they are collaborating. Yet many designers underestimate the depth and breadth of skill and knowledge required by those who survive in very challenging conditions of deprivation. Without the establishment of mutual respect and equality of exchanges between designer and collaborating persons, little of lasting value can easily be achieved.

By establishing a partnership, motivating confidence in all participants for expressing their own ideas as part of the design process, learning becomes part of the operation for all involved.

Should design for development be pursued outside, or within, the market-driven consumerist economic system?

In terms of manufacturing, whether by hand or computerized machine, the global model for design and marketing processes has evolved over many years to very sophisticated levels. But the basic questions remain:

— Where are the customers?

— What are their ever-changing needs and desires?

— Where is the competitor?

— What are they making?

— How much can be charged for a product?

— What new techniques can be developed or used to improve the function or quality of the product?

— How is the product or service to be sold to the customer?

These questions remain constant to a great degree, regardless of whether a product or service is sold through fair trade or mainstream commercial systems. To work effectively as a manufacturer commercially, it is necessary to know the answers to such questions.

Do development projects require a different design process?

Designers also work within communities on social development projects that benefit in non-commercial ways. But the nature of the design process is the same. Who is trying to do what for whom, why and how are they doing it? In the course of involvement in any development project, a designer becomes a composite of listener, counsellor, catalyst, facilitator, moderator, information resource and search engine, educator, student, technician, researcher, production systems adviser, office clerk, quality controller, sociologist, social psychologist, participant, manager, maker, salesperson, writer, champion, evaluator.

This is not necessarily so in mainstream commercial design activity. A designer has to be prepared to learn additional skills, study a wide range of new and sometimes challenging information and, most importantly, learn to play a supporting rather than a leading role in the project owner's activity. If design intervention is to be sustainable, then the individual, community or group must be the owner of the programme. The designer's role is to help them achieve their goal, in any way they can, and then walk away.

Conclusion

The design community – made up
of all those engaged in design and
designing – is increasingly conscious
of the sustainability agenda. Designers
are beginning to move towards a better
understanding of what they can do to
address sustainability, and how they
can effectively respond to it through
design. Design has a crucial part to
play in addressing sustainability. As a
result, the roles and responsibilities of
designers are changing.

Our thinking is becoming more
sophisticated about the ways in which
design and sustainability interrelate.
The words design and sustainability are
not fixed in their meaning, and neither
is the emerging language of design
for sustainability. What is undeniable
is that the sustainability agenda is
asking fundamental questions of design
and designers. Sustainability should
ultimately define our world view, and
everything we design should contribute
to delivering that sustainability-led
world view.

Designers globally are reacting to this challenge in diverse and inspiring ways. What is apparent is that their approach is increasingly knowing, interdisciplinary, and socially networked. What is now needed is discussion of what makes an effective and successful project in these diverse and broad arenas. Do we need some shared principles, practices and standards for undertaking and evaluating design for sustainability projects? How such initiatives are undertaken is also crucial in regard to valuing local knowledge and being human-centred but still responding to global themes. This is of particular importance for those working within relatively new agendas for design such as overcoming poverty.

In addition, there needs to be enhanced dialogue and the sharing of experiences in setting up and undertaking design for sustainable change projects and organizations. This would hopefully lead to a greater understanding of the supportive infrastructures and funding routes available and required to successfully harness design.

We need to understand the core strategic and practical skills and knowledge required to successfully address the various sustainability agendas through design at a large as well as small-scale level. Then we can begin to develop and deliver it through, amongst other opportunities, multi-disciplinary higher educational and life-long learning provision, internships and collaborative research.

There are new opportunities for design and designers to address these agendas but we need to firm up on the details and practicalities of how designers and design can be most effective in how and what they do.

This arena is new to most designers. We have an obligation to teach design students the new skills and knowledge they will need to operate within the increasingly broad realm of design for sustainability. Existing professional designers need to recognize that their existing skill-set may not be adequate for these new challenges.

This includes expertise such as the ability to influence social policy through leadership and negotiation. In whatever way we aim to bring about design for sustainable change, it takes patience, skill and diplomacy. Design needs to change. Designers themselves need to change. Only then are we likely to see design for sustainable change on a significant scale.

Design needs to change. Designers themselves need to change. Only then are we likely to see design for sustainable change on a significant scale.

Bibliography

Armstrong, William; Borg, Johan; Krizack, Marc; Lindsley, Alida; Mines, Kylie; Pearlman, Jon; Reisinger, Kim; Sarah Sheldon (2008) Guidelines on the provision of Manual Wheelchairs in Less Resourced Settings. Geneva: World Health Organization, WHO Press. (www.wheelchairsforafrica.org/documents/WHOGUIDELINES.pdf)

Balaram, Singanapalli (2009) Design in India: The Importance of the Ahmedabad Declaration. *Design Issues*. August, Volume 25, Number 4.

Bloemink, Barbara (2007) *Design for the Other 90% catalogue.* New York: Cooper-Hewitt, National Design Museum.

Brown, Tim (2009) *Change by Design: How Design Thinking Transforms Organizations and Inspires Innovation.* New York: HarperBusiness.

Buchanan, Richard (1992) Wicked Problems in Design Thinking. *Design Issues*, Vol. 8. No. 2 (Spring).

Burns, Colin; Vanstone, Chris; and Winhall, Jennie (2006) Transformation Design. *RED PAPER 02*. London: Design Council.

Chapman, Jonathan and Gant, Nick (2007) *Designers, Visionaries and Other Stories*. London: Earthscan.

Darnton, Andrew (2004) *Driving Public Behaviours for Sustainable Lifestyles (Report 2)*. London: Department for Environment, Food and Rural Affairs.

Department for Culture, Media and Sport, UK (1998) *Creative Industries Mapping Document 1998*. London: DCMS.

Department of Trade and Industry (2003) *Competing in The Global Economy: The Innovation Challenge*. London: DTI.

Eames, Charles and Eames, Ray (1958) *India Report*. New Delhi: Government of India.

Elkington, John (1997) *Cannibals with Forks: The Triple Bottom Line of 21st Century Business*. Oxford: Capstone.

Fuad-Luke, Alastair (2009) *Design Activism: Beautiful Strangeness for a Sustainable World*. London: Earthscan.

Goggin, Philip (1996) Glossary: Key Concepts and Definitions. *The Interdisciplinary Journal of Design and Contextual Studies, Co-design*, Vol. 01/02/03.

Heskett, John (2005) *Design: A Very Short Introduction*. Oxford: Oxford University Press.

Hnatow, Marilyn (2009) *Aid to Artisans: Building Profitable Craft Businesses*. United States Agency International Development. Business Growth Initiative Project. (www.businessgrowthinitiative.org)

Holme, Richard and Watts, Phil (2000) *Corporate Social Responsibility: Making Good Business Sense*. Conches-Geneva, Switzerland: World Business Council for Sustainable Development.

Hopkins, Rob (2008) *The Transition Handbook: From Oil Dependency to Local Resilience*. Totnes, Devon: Green Books.

IDEO. (2009) Human Centered Design Toolkit. (www.ideo.com/work/human-centered-design-toolkit/)

Jones, John Chris (1992) *Design Methods*. 2nd ed. London: Chapman & Hall.

Kelley, Tom (2001) *The Art of Innovation*. New York: Currency/Doubleday.

Kemp, Klaus and Ueki-Polet, Keiko (2010) *Less and More: The Design Ethos of Dieter Rams*. Bilingual edition. Berlin / London: Die Gestalten Verlag.

Korten, David C. (1999) *The Post-Corporate World: Life after Capitalism*. San Francisco, CA: Berrett-Koehler.

Lovelock, James (2007) *The Revenge of Gaia*. London: Penguin.

Løvlie, Lavrans; Downs, Chris; Reason, Ben. Bottom-line Experiences: Measuring the Value of Design in Service. *Design Management Review* (Winter 2008).

Manzini, Ezio (2001) Sustainability and Scenario Building: Scenarios of Sustainable Wellbeing and Sustainable Solutions Development. Paper presented at Ecodesign 2001, Tokyo, Japan.

Manzini, Ezio and Jegou, François (2003) Sustainable Everyday — Scenarios, Visions, Possible Worlds. *Design Philosophy Papers* Issue 4. (www.changedesign.org/Resources/Manzini/Manuscripts/ScenariosSummary.pdf)

Margolin, Victor (1998) Design for a Sustainable World. *Design Issues*, Summer. Volume 14, Number 2.

Margolin, Victor (2007) Design for Development: Towards a History. *Design Studies*. Volume 28.

Maslow, Abraham (1943) A Theory of Human Motivation. *Psychological Review*. Volume 50.

Mason, Tania (2004) Newsmaker: Mr Motivator - David Constantine, Co-founder, Motivation. *Third Sector*. 7 April.

Matsuura, Koi-chiro (2001) *Universal Declaration on Cultural Diversity*. Paris: UNESCO.

Max-Neef, Manfred A. (1991) *Human Scale Development: Conception, Application and Further Reflections*. New York and London: The Apex Press.

McDonough, William and Braungart, Michael (2002) *Cradle to Cradle: Remaking the Way We Make Things*. New York: North Point Press.

Miller, Lindsay, Dawans, Vincent and Alter, Kim (2009) *Industree Craft: A Case Study in Social Enterprise Development Using the Four Lenses Approach*. Virtue Ventures. (www.4lenses.org/files/industree_craft_4lenses_v1.pdf)

Moholy-Nagy, László (1947) *Vision in Motion*. Chicago: Institute of Design.

Mulgan, Geoff (2007) *Social Innovation: What It Is, Why It Matters, and How It Can Be Accelerated*. Oxford: Skoll Centre for Social Entrepreneurship, University of Oxford.

Myerson, Jeremy (2007) Pressing the Pause Button. Closing remarks at Intersections 07 conference. (www.designcouncil.org.uk)

Papanek, Victor (1971, 1984) *Design for the Real World: Human Ecology and Social Change*. 2nd edition. London: Thames and Hudson.

Porritt, Jonathon (2007) *Capitalism as if the World Matters*. Revised edition. London: Earthscan.

Potter, Norman (2008) *What Is a Designer: Things, Places, Messages*. 4th revised edition. London: Hyphen Press.

Ramsay Merriam, Caroline (1999) Characteristics of World Trade in Crafts. Silver Spring: CHF International.

Rule, Alix (2008) The Revolution Will Not Be Designed. 11 January. (www.inthesetimes.com/article/3464/the_revolution_will_not_be_designed)

Sheldon S, Jacobs NA, eds. (2006) Report of a Consensus Conference on Wheelchairs for Developing Countries, Bangalore, India, 6–11 November 2006. Copenhagen, International Society for Prosthetics and Orthotics. (http://pdf.usaid.gov/pdf_docs/PNADP827.pdf)

Simon, Herbert (1969) *Sciences of the Artificial*. Cambridge, MA: MIT Press.

Stairs, David (2005) Altruism as Design Methodology. *Design Issues*, Volume 21, Number 2 (Spring).

Stairs, David (2009) Arguing with Success (http://design-altruism-project.org/?p=90)

Stairs, David (2007) Why Design Won't Save the World. (www.designobserver.com/observatory/entry.html?entry=5777)

Thackara, John (2005) *In the Bubble: Designing in a Complex World*. Cambridge, MA: MIT Press

Thackara, John (2007) *Designers, Visionaries and Other Stories*. London: Earthscan.

Thackara, John (2007) *Wouldn't it be Great If...* (Dott 07 manual). London: Design Council.

Thorpe, Ann (2007) *The Designer's Atlas of Sustainability*. Washington, DC: Island Press.

United Nations Conference on Trade and Development (2008) *Creative Economy Report 2008: The Challenge of Assessing the Creative Economy Towards Informed Policy-making*.

United Nations Convention on the Rights of Persons with Disabilities: Some Facts about Persons with Disabilities (2007) (www.un.org/disabilities/convention/facts.shtml)

United Nations Educational, Scientific and Cultural Organisation's (UNESCO) Decade of Education for Sustainable Development (ESD). (www.unesco.org/en/esd/decade-of-esd/)

United Nations General Assembly (1986) *Declaration on the Right to Development: resolution / adopted by the General Assembly*, 4 December, A/RES/41/128. (www.globalissues.org/article/559/united-nations-world-summit-2005)

United Nations General Assembly (2005) *World Summit Outcome*. (www.globalissues.org/article/559/united-nations-world-summit-2005)

United Nations Population Fund (2007) *State of World Population 2007: Unleashing the Potential of Urban Growth*. (www.unfpa.org/swp/2007/presskit/pdf/sowp2007_eng.pdf).

Walker, Stuart (2006) *Sustainable by Design: Explorations in Theory and Practice*. London: Earthscan.

Walters, Helen (2009) Inside the Design Thinking Process. www.businessweek.com. 14 December.

We Are What We Do (2004) *Change the World for a Fiver*. London: Short Books.

Whiteley. Nigel (1993) *Design for Society*. London: Reaktion Books.

Wilkinson, Richard and Pickett, Kate (2009) *The Spirit Level: Why More Equal Societies Almost Always Do Better*. London: Allen Lane.

World Commission on Environment and Development (1987) *Our Common Future*. Oxford: Oxford University Press. [The Brundtland report]

World Bank, The (2007) *Agriculture for Development*. World Development Report 2008. Washington, DC: The International Bank for Reconstruction and Development / The World Bank

World Bank, The (2008) *2008 World Development Indicators: Poverty data: A supplement to World Development Indicators*. Washington: International Bank for Reconstruction and Development / The World Bank.

Note: all online resources accessed 1 December 2010.

Further resources

A growing number of books and journal articles examine sustainable design or design for sustainability in different ways (as shown by their titles). Below are those that we know students and practitioners have found useful. Also included are useful sources on sustainable living and sustainable development.

Bhamra, Tracy and Lofthouse, Vicky (2007) *Design for Sustainability: A Practical Approach*. Farnham: Gower.

Chapman, Jonathan (2005) *Emotionally Durable Design: Objects, Experiences and Empathy*. London: Earthscan.

Chapman, Jonathan and Gant, Nick, ed. (2007) *Designers, Visionaries and Other Stories: A Collection of Sustainable Design Essays*. London: Earthscan.

Charter, Martin and Tischner, Ursula (2001) *Sustainable Solutions: Developing Products and Services for the Future*. Sheffield: Greenleaf.

Datschefski, Edwin (2001) *The Total Beauty of Sustainable Products*. London: RotoVision.

Desai, Pooran and Riddlestone, Sarah (2007) *Schumacher Briefings: Bioregional Solutions: For Living on One Planet*. Totnes: Green Books.

Dougherty, Brian and Celery Design (2008) *Green Graphic Design*. New York: Allworth Press.

Dresner, Simon (2002) *The Principles of Sustainability*. London: Earthscan.

Fletcher, Kate (2008) *Sustainable Fashion and Textiles: Design Journeys*. London: Earthscan.

Fry, Tony (2008) *Design Futuring: Sustainability, Ethics and New Practice*. Oxford: Berg.

Fuad-Luke, Alastair (2009) *The Eco-Design Handbook: A Complete Sourcebook for the Home and Office*. Third edition. London: Thames & Hudson.

Grant, John (2010) *Co-opportunity: Join Up for a Sustainable, Resilient, Prosperous World*. Oxford: John Wiley & Sons, Inc.

Mackenzie, Dorothy (1991) *Green Design: Design for the Environment*. London: Laurence King.

Margolin. Victor (1998) Design for a Sustainable World. *Design Issues*. Vol. 14, No. 2, pp. 83–92. MIT Press.

Margolin. Victor (2007) Design for Development: Towards a History. *Design Studies*. Vol. 28, Issue 2, pp. 111–115. MIT Press.

Margolin, Victor and Margolin, Sylvia (2002) A 'Social Model' of Design: Issues of Practice and Research. *Design Issues*. Vol. 18, No. 4, pp. 24–30. MIT Press.

McDonough, William and Braungart, Michael (2002) *Cradle to Cradle: Remaking the Way We Make Things*. New York: North Point Press.

Papanek, Victor (1984) *Design for the Real World: Human Ecology and Social Change*. 2nd edition. London: Thames & Hudson.

Papanek, Victor (1995) *The Green Imperative: Ecology and ethics in design and architecture*. London: Thames & Hudson.

Roberts, Lucienne (2006) *Good: An Introduction to Ethics in Graphic Design*. Worthing: AVA Academia.

Shedroff, Nathan (2009) *Design is the Problem: The Future of Design Must be Sustainable*. New York: Rosenfeld Media.

Thackara, John (2005) *In the Bubble: Designing in a Complex World*. Cambridge, MA: MIT Press.

Thorpe, Ann (2007) *The Designer's Atlas of Sustainability*. Washington, DC: Island Press.

Walker, Stuart (2006) *Sustainable by Design: Explorations in Theory and Practice*. London: Earthscan.

Whiteley, Nigel (1993) *Design For Society*. London: Reaktion Books.

Wood, John (2007) *Design for Micro-utopias: Making the Unthinkable Possible*. Farnham: Gower.

Featured organizations

www.acmeclimateaction.com

www.adbusters.org

www.aidtoartisans.org

www.architectureforhumanity.org

www.bioregional.com

www.cabe.org.uk/case-studies/bedzed

www.celerydesign.com/eco-tools

www.changinghabbits.co.uk

www.core77.com

www.creativecommons.org

www.crisis.org.uk

www.d4s-de.org

www.defra.gov.uk

www.desis-network.org

www.designactivism.net

www.designactivism.org

www.design-altruism-project.org

www.designcouncil.org.uk

www.designerswithoutborders.org

www.designforsocialimpact.com

www.designforthefirstworld.com

www.candesignmakeadifference.com/about/

www.desis-network.org

www.diykyoto.com

www.dott07.com

www.dottcornwall.com/

en.wikipedia.org/wiki/Vélib'

www.enginegroup.co.uk

www.foldschool.com

www.forumforthefuture.org

www.fosterandpartners.com

www.freeplayenergy.com

www.fuad-luke.com

www.greenlivingpedia.org/Freiburg

www.greenmap.org

www.happyplanetindex.org

www.hermanmiller.co.uk

hdr.undp.org/en

hdr.undp.org/en/statistics

www.ideastore.co.uk

www.ideo.com/work

www.interfaceglobal.com

www.ikat.org

industree.org.in

www.mbdc.com

www.motivation.org.uk

other90.cooperhewitt.org

www.opengreenmap.org

plana.marksandspencer.com

www.planestupid.com

www.provokateur.com

www.remarkable.co.uk

www.shapersw.net

www.streetcar.co.uk

www.sustainability.com

www.sustainableminds.com

www.sustainable-everyday.net

www.thirdsector.co.uk

www.transitiontowns.org/Brixton

www.treehugger.com

www.unesco.org/en/esd/decade-of-esd

www.undp.org/en/statistics

www.velib.paris.fr

www.wearewhatwedo.org

www.wemake.co.uk

www.wewanttap.com

www.zedfactory.com

Online resources

www.cfsd.org.uk
The Centre for Sustainable Design
facilitates discussion and research on
ecodesign and broader sustainability
considerations in product and service
development. This is achieved through
training, workshops, conferences,
research, consultancy, publications, and
the Internet. The centre also acts as an
information clearing house and a focus
for innovative thinking on sustainable
products and services.

www.d4s-de.org
This Design for Sustainability (D4S)
manual is targeted at small- and
medium-sized enterprises (SMEs)
especially in emerging and developing
countries. The resource was drafted
by the Design for Sustainability (DfS)
Programme at Delft University of
Technology, for UNEP's Production and
Consumption Unit of the Division of
Technology, Industry and Economics.
The manual can be downloaded for free
from the above website.

www.designersaccord.org
The Designers Accord is a global
coalition of designers, educators and
business leaders working together
to create positive environmental and
social impact. It was founded with the
goal of changing the way the creative
community does business. They
provide a participatory platform with
online and offline 'manifestations'
so that members have access to
a community of peers who share
methodologies, resources, and
experiences around environmental
and social issues in design. To be an
individual member you have to declare
your intention to support the Designers
Accord. All adopters, supporters
and endorsers follow a basic code of
conduct: 'Do no harm; communicate
and collaborate; keep learning, keep
teaching; instigate meaningful change;
make theory action'.

http://designactivism.net/
The design activism weblog is the
creation of Ann Thorpe and stems
from her work on sustainable design,
particularly her book *The Designer's
Atlas of Sustainability*. She states that
to 'design effectively for a cause, such
as sustainability, designers have to
become activists to a certain extent.
Explicit activism has been largely
taboo among designers'. This resource
explores design as activism and its
relationship to sustainable design.

www.demi.org.uk
This website contains lots of
information on design for sustainability.
You can explore it by clicking on the
map that shows this information
clustered in six sectors. demi has been
written, unless otherwise stated, by
researchers at Goldsmiths College,
University of London as part of a UK
Government-funded project.

www.inhabitat.com
Inhabitat.com is a weblog 'devoted
to the future of design, tracking the
innovations in technology, practices
and materials that are pushing
architecture and home design towards
a smarter and more sustainable
future'. Inhabitat's attention is focused
on objects and spaces that are eco-
friendly, multi-purpose, modular
and/or interactive. This weblog was
started through a frustration with
what magazines touted as 'good
design', which was all style and no
substance. Inhabitat are also frustrated
at 'seeing an emerging category called
"Green Design" – as if sustainability
is somehow separate from good
design in general. We believe that all
design should be inherently "Green".
Good design is not about colour,
style or trends – but instead about
thoughtfully considering the user, the
experience, the social context and the
impact of an object on the surrounding
environment.'

www.livingprinciples.org
The Living Principles for Design website
aims to 'guide purposeful action,
celebrate and popularize the efforts of
those who use design thinking to create
positive cultural change'. The website
is 'the place where we co-create,
share and showcase best practices,
tools, stories and ideas for enabling
sustainable action across all design
disciplines'.

www.o2.org
O2 Global Network is an international
not-for-profit organization that
promotes ecological principles
and sustainable design practices
internationally. It is an informal
network comprising O2 Global Network
foundation; regional O2 Hubs; local
O2 Groups; O2 Liaisons and individual
members. There are regional/country
Hubs: Europe (Southeast), India,
Nordic, Switzerland, UK and USA. The
O2 Global Network website provides
sustainable design news; mailing lists;
O2 Liaison officers' contact details;
and resources such as recommended
books, tools and case studies.

www.sustainable-everyday.net
The Sustainable Everyday Project (SEP)
is an open-web platform that aims
to stimulate discussion on possible
sustainable futures. The SEP platform
hosts several research activities and
workshop activities. The platform is
an organization and communication
tool providing an open-web space
and showcase for activities relating to
design and sustainability in everyday
contexts. One of the initiatives is DESIS
(Design for Social Innovation and
Sustainability), a network of schools of
design and other schools, institutions,
companies and non-profit organizations
interested in promoting and supporting
design for social innovation and
sustainability. There are a growing
number of sub-networks within a
specified local area called DESIS-Local.
They coordinate themselves via DESIS-
International, the framework for global
initiatives and communications.

www.treehugger.com
TreeHugger is the leading media outlet
dedicated to driving sustainability into
the mainstream. Partial to a modern
aesthetic, it strives to be a one-stop
shop for green news, solutions and
product information. Blogs, weekly
and daily newsletters, weekly radio
interviews and regularly updated
Twitter and Facebook pages are
published. They have a specialist
design and architecture editor and
a section dedicated to Design for
Sustainability.

www.unep.fr/scp
The Sustainable Consumption and
Production (SCP) branch of the United
Nations Environment Programme's
(UNEP) Division of Technology,
Industry and Economics focuses on
achieving increased understanding
and implementation by public and
private decision-makers of policies
and actions for SCP. They have
produced some excellent resources and
publications that are free and generally
downloadable from this website.

www.worldchanging.com
Worldchanging.com is a non-profit
media organization with headquarters
in Seattle that comprises a global
network of independent journalists,
designers and thinkers. They cover
the world's innovative solutions to the
planet's problems and inspire readers
around the world with stories of new
tools, models and ideas for building a
bright, green future. They have covered
issues such as refugee aid, renewable
energy and innovative solutions for
improving building, transportation,
communication and quality of life.
They claim to have produced 'more
than 11,000 visionary articles and one
best-selling book, and [have] become
a go-to source for forward-thinking,
solutions-based journalism that takes a
big-picture approach to sustainability'.

Index

Page numbers in *italics* refer to
illustrations.

3 pillars model of sustainable
development 82
3 Rs (reduce, reuse, recycle) model 104
3BL (Triple Bottom Line) model 92–3
5 Capitals model 94–5
30 St Mary Axe ('Gherkin') *21*

Acme Climate Action campaign 31
action models 18–19
activism 56–73, 172
Adbusters 64–5
advertising parodies *64*, 65
AfH (Architecture for Humanity) 52–3,
69, 160–1
Aid to Artisans (ATA) 150–1
altruism 66–7, 69, 73
Ambedker Nager Community Centre,
India *52*
anti-advertising *64*, 65
Architecture for Humanity (AfH) 52–3,
69, 160–1
art 17
artisans 150–1, 152, *164*
ATA (Aid to Artisans) 150–1
attitudes 24–5
aviation expansion, campaigns against
61, 63

bags *90*, 91, 121
Ballyn, John 164–5
banners *29*
Beddington Zero Energy Development
(BedZED) 126–7
behaviour 120–1
bibliography 168–9
bike hire schemes 123
billboards 64, *65*
BioRegional 88–9, 126, 127
Biyani, Kishore 152
Blackburn, Joshua 30–1
Bloemink, Barbara 155
blogs 172, 173
book design 31
bottled water 31
boxes *29*
Brawer, Wendy 129
Brazil 99
Brixton, London 136–7
Brixton Pound (B£) *136–7*
Brown, Tim 36, 39
Brundtland Report 78
build phase, co-creation 49
business ethics 53, 112, *114*
Buy Fresh Buy Local campaign 70

capital models 92–5
car sharing 44–5, 115
carbon emissions 141
cardboard furniture *51*
carpet tiles 113
Carter, Ennis 70–1
categories of design 17, 23
Celery Design 26–9

Central Asia Institute 69
Centre for Sustainable Design 172
chairs *51*, 111
challenges 36–7
charities 149, 161
Chhiber, Neelam 152
child labour 93
China 99
Chocolatl packaging *29*
Christmas project (Crisis) 160–1
cigarette advertising, subversion of *64*
cities 134–5
climate change *80*
co-creation 47, 49
co-delivery 39
co-design 39, 47, 48
co-discovery 38
collaboration 60
communities 89, 126–7
community centres *52*
community learning resource centres
67, 72–3
community programmes 89
competitions 163
concentric circles model, sustainable
development 82, *83*
concept sketches *21*
Constable, John *78*, 79
Constantine, David 156, 157
consumer behaviour 125
corporate social responsibility (CSR)
53, 112, *114*
Costa Rica 87
Cradle to Cradle design protocol 110
craft 17, 20, 24, 55, 150–3
Creative Commons 50–1
creative groups 133
creativity cards 41
Crisis Christmas project 160–1
CSR (corporate social responsibility)
53, 112, *114*
cultural diversity 83
culture jamming *64*, 65
currencies *136–7*
cycle hire schemes 123

D-Rev 150
D4S (Design for Sustainability) 172
Darnton, Andrew 124
day centres 161
design
    action models 18–19
    activism 56–73, 172
    altruism 66–7, 69, 73
    and art 17
    as attitude 24–5
    categories 17, 23
    challenges 36–7
    concepts 20–1
    and craft 17, 20, 55, 150
    developing countries 148–51
    for development 142–65
    Dieter Rams' principles 116

as a field 16–17
history 17
industry 17
innovations 32–3
inspiration tools 40–1
management 17
models 20, 33
new roles 33
open source 50–1
outcomes 22–3, 35
participation 33, 39, 46–9, *67*
as political act 23
principles 116
process models 18–19
professionalism 25
proposals 20–1
realization 20
roles 141
scope 24–5, 55
sector 16
strategic value 27
studies 17
sustainability
    47, 72, 102–17, 133, 166–7, 172
sustainable living 118–41
'T'-shaped model 33
thinking 24, 34–55
tools 40–1, 108, 109, *158–9*
values 19
Design Council 39
Design for the First World 162–3
Design for the Other 90, *154*, 155
Design for Social Impact (DfSI) 70–1
Design for Social Innovation and
Sustainability (DESIS) 133, 172
Design for Sustainability (D4S) 172
design-orienting scenarios (DOS) 131
Designers Accord 172
Designers without Borders (DWB) 69
Designs of the Time (Dott) 38–9, 140–1
DESIS (Design for Social Innovation and
Sustainability) 133, 172
developed countries 163
developing countries *80, 81*, 99, 125
    craft products 150–3
    Design for the First World 163
    design interventions 148–51
development 142–65
DfSI (Design for Social Impact) 70–1
diagnosis phase, projects 38
disabled people 156, 157
DIY Kyoto *120*
DOS (design-orienting scenarios) 131
Dott (Designs of the Time) 38–9, 140–1
DWB (Designers without Borders) 69

Eames, Charles and Ray 145
eco-design 106–9
eco-effectiveness 109, 110
eco-efficiency 109
ecological footprints 86, *87*
economic capital 93
economic development 99

effectiveness 109
efficiency 109
electricity meters *120*, 121
Elephant Pharmacy *29*
energy-efficient light bulbs 121
energy meters *120*, 121
Engine 48–9
England 139
enterprise model 149–51
envelopes *28*
environmental impacts
    27, 80, 81, *87*, 106–9
ethical business 53, 112, *114*
ethical communications 30
Europe 99, 112
exhibitions 25, 155
expertise 33

farmers' markets *70, 132, 133*
Feeding Milan project *132, 133*
financial capital 95
Five Capitals model 94–5
flooring tiles 113
Flowmaker 40–1
Foldschool furniture *51*
food campaigns *70*
Forum for the Future 94, 98, *99*
Foster, Norman 21
France 123
Freeplay Indigo Lantern *22*
Freiburg, Germany 135
Fuad-Luke, Alastair 59
furniture *51*, 111
further reading 170

Gaia theory 79
GDP (Gross Domestic Product) 144, 145
generalisms 33
Germany 135
'Gherkin' office building *21*
Goggin, Philip 106
graphic design 26–9, 43, *70*
grass-roots innovation 141
green cities 135
green design 104–5
Green Maps *128*, 129
green politics 99
Greenpeace *61*
Gross Domestic Product (GDP) 144, 145

Habbits *87*
handbags *90*
Happy Planet Index (HPI) 87
The Hay Wain (Constable) *78*, 79
HCD (Human-Centered Design) Toolkit
158–9
HDI (Human Development Index)
84–5, 145
Heathrow Airport, London *61*
Herman Miller Inc. 111
Hewlett Packard (HP) *29*
hierarchy of needs 146

Hindmarch, Anya *90*
hire schemes 123
history of design 17
holistic design 43, 126
homeless people 160–1
housing projects 126–7
HP (Hewlett Packard) *29*
HPI (Happy Planet Index) 87
human capital 93, 95
Human-Centered Design (HCD) Toolkit
    158–9, 159
Human Development Index (HDI)
    84–5, 145
human needs 146–7
Human Scale Development 147

ICF (Industree Crafts Foundation) 152–3
Ideas Sharing Stall *132*
identify phase, co-creation 49
IDEO 158–9
incremental change 55, 63
India *52*, 152
indices of sustainability 84–7
Industree Crafts Foundation (ICF) 152–3
inequalities 144–5
Inhabitat 172
innovations 32–3, 114–17, 155
inspiration tools 40–1
interactive books 31
Interface 113
interviews
    Anne Thorpe 72–3
    David Stairs 68–9
    Ezio Manzini 132–3
    John Ballyn 164–5
    Jonathon Porritt 98–9
    Joshua Blackburn 30–1
irrigation *150*
Italy *132, 133*

Janz, Wes 66
'Joe Chemo' parody *64*

Kasturi, Poonam Bir 152
Koïchiro Matsuura 83

lanterns *22*
LCA (life cycle assessments) 108, 109
leasing models 113, 121
Leeds Festival of Design Activism 58
legacies 39
letterheads *28*
libraries *72–3*
licensing systems 50–1
life cycle assessments (LCA) 108, 109
life cycles of products 106–9, 113
LifeStraw *154*
lifestyles 91, 124–33
light bulbs 121
live|work 45
Living Principles for Design 172
local currencies *136–7*, 137
local design 150

local solutions 53, *70*
localization 136, 145
logotypes *50, 88, 99*
London *61, 72–3*, 136–7
Lovelock, James 79
low-energy light bulbs 121

Mager, Birgit 42
Mallari, Albert John *67*
manufacturing 95, 107, 165
Manzini, Ezio 130, 132–3
maps *128*, 129, *162*
Marks & Spencer *114*
Maslow, Abraham 146
material cycles 110, 111
Max-Neef, Manfred 147
Merriam, Caroline Ramsay 151
Milan *132, 133*
mineral water 31
Missouri 71
modelling 20
Moholy-Nagy, László 25
Mother Earth 152, *153*
Motivation 156–7
Myerson, Jeremy 55

natural capital 93, 95
needs, designing for 146–7
Nehru, Jawaharlal 145
New York City *128*, 129
NGOs (non-governmental
    organizations) 159
No Derivative Works 50
non-governmental organizations
    (NGOs) 159
non-profit sector 71
Norman, Donald 54

O2 Global Network 172
office furniture 111
'One Planet Communities' programme
    89
One Planet Living 88–9
online resources 172–3
open architecture 53
open source design 50–1
organization websites 171
outcomes 22–3, 35
overlapping circles model, sustainable
    development *83*

packaging design *29*
Papanek, Victor 67, 147, 148
paper 26–7
paperboard boxes *29*
Paris 123
parodies of advertising *64*, 65
participatory design 33, 39, 46–9, *67*
pencils 105 performance purchasing
121
Philippines *67*
Pickett, Kate 145
pizza delivery, service design 43

Plan A, Marks & Spencer 114
Plane Stupid *63*
plastic bags 90, 91, 121
plastics 27
political acts 23, 65
political cultures 99
Porritt, Jonathon 94, 98–9
poverty alleviation 81, 147, 149–51
problem-setting/solving 38–9
process models 18–19
product life cycles 106–9, 113
product ownership 121
Product Service Systems (PSS) 113, 121,
122
professionalism 25, 60
progress 79
project phases 38–9
Provokateur 30–1
PSS (Product Service Systems) 113, 121,
122
public sector 37

Rams, Dieter 116
realization of design 20
recycled design 104, 105
recycled materials 91, 105, 111
reduce, reuse, recycle (3Rs) model 104
reforms 73
regional sustainability 138–41
Remarkable Pencils Ltd 105
residential centres 161
resource efficiency 109
resources 170–3
Rule, Alix 55

Sachs, Jeffrey 149
'Save Our Roots' campaign 71
scenarios for sustainable living 130–1
scepticism 55
schools 73
scope of design 24–5, 55
SCP (Sustainable Consumption and
Production) 173
SEP (Sustainable Everyday Project) 172
service design 23, 42–3, 48–9, 122
sexual health project *140*
shared ownership 121
shared visions 47
shopping bags *90*, 91, 121
signs 29
Silver Surfer lessons *72–3*
Simon, Herbert 47
single issues 91, 104–5
sketches *21*
'skulling' 64
smoking, anti-advertising *64*
social capital 95
social development projects 165
social innovations 33, 125, 133, 141
societal challenges 36–7
Sonoma Mountain Village (US) 89
South West of England 139
specialisms 33, 43

The Spirit Level (Wilkinson and Pickett)
    145
Stairs, David 68–9
stakeholders 46–7, 92
stationery *28*, 105
strategic value 27
Streetcar 44–5
subversion of advertising *64*, 65
supermarkets *114*
sustainability 75–99
    behaviour 120–1
    cities 134–5
    communities 126–7
    definition 78
    and design
        47, 72, 102–17, 133, 166–7, 172
    development
        78–9, 80–3, 85–7, 92–5, 98–9
    indices 84–7
    lifestyles 91, 124–33
    measurement 84–9
    models 80–3
    as modern myth 97
    regions 138–41
    single issues 91
    societies 115
    systems 122
    use of term 97, 98
Sustainability Scorecard *27*
Sustainability South West (England) 139
Sustainable Consumption and
Production (SCP) 173
Sustainable Everyday Project (SEP) 172
Sustainable Minds 109
Swiss Re Building ('Gherkin') *21*
systems design 122

'T'-shaped model 33
Tan, Lauren 141
Thackara, John 47, 105
Thorpe, Anne 60, 72–3, 79, 115
three pillars model of sustainable
    development 82
three Rs (reduce, reuse, recycle) model
    104
tools 40–1
    Human-Centered Design Toolkit
        158–9
    life cycle assessments 108, 109
traditional crafts 151
transformation design 37, 55
Transition Towns 136–7
transport
    car sharing 44–5, 115
    cycle hire schemes 123
treadle pumps *150*
TreeHugger 173
Triple Bottom Line (3BL) model 92–3

UK 126–7, 136–7, 139, 141, 160–1
UNESCO (United Nations Educational,
    Scientific and Cultural Organization)
    81

United Nations Human Development
   Index (HDI) *84–5*, 145
United States *70*, 89, 99, 112, 129
urban planning 135
use not own models 121
user participation *48*

values 19
Vélib' cycle hire scheme 123

Walker, Stuart 96, 97
Walters, Helen 55
waste management model 104
water 31, *154*
Wattson energy meters *120*
We Want Tap campaign *30*, 31
weblogs 172, 173
websites 171–3
wheelchairs 156–7
Whitechapel Idea Store *72–3*
Wilkinson, Richard 145
wind-up lanterns *22*
women's empowerment 151
World Commission on Environment and
Development 81
Worldchanging.com 173
Worldmade Wheelchair Services 157

Young Foundation 125

Compiled by
Indexing Specialists (UK) Ltd

Picture credits

Chapter 1

21
Sketch of the Gherkin © Norman Foster/Foster + Partners.

22
Indigo lantern © Freeplay Energy UK Ltd.

26–29
Ecological Guide to Paper; Sustainability Scorecard; Is it a letterhead or an envelope?; Hewlett Packard communication; Elephant Pharmacy Banners; Chocolatl packaging © Celery Design Collaborative.

30–31
Acme Climate Action book and We Want Tap courtesy of Provokateur.

Chapter 2

40–41
Flowmaker design creativity cards © WEmake.

43
Pizza delivery leaflet © Marish. Courtesy of Shutterstock.com

44–45
Streetcar image courtesy of Streetcar Limited.

46
Participatory design illustration by Penny Goodwin.

48–49
Engine Design Process and User Participation © Engine Service Design 2007.

50
Creative Commons logos courtesy of Creativecommons.org.

51
Fold School images courtesy of Nicola Enrico © foldschool 2007. Pictures by Rolf Kueng www. kuengfu.ch.

53
Ambedker Nager Community Centre image courtesy of Architecture for Humanity.

54
The Emperor's New Clothes, the court admiring the Emperor's costume, by Hans Christian Andersen, 1805–75, from Fairy Tales published between 1835–72. Artist: Harry Clark: 1890–1931. Courtesy of The Art Archive / Bibliothèque des Arts Décoratifs Paris / Gianni Dagli Orti.

Chapter 3

61
Heathrow Plane Protest © Greenpeace.

62–63
Plane Stupid's cinema trailer *Your Flight has an Impact*. Written and commissioned by creative agency Mother and made by production company Rattling Stick. Director Daniel Kleinman.

64
Joe Chemo Bed Spoof courtesy of Adbusters Media Foundation.

67
Community learning resource centres, all images from Edukasyon para sa Kinabukasan Incorporated (Eduk, Inc.), Quezon City, Philippines.

68
David Stairs photograph by Sydnee MacKay.

68–69
Kashmiri refugees in school, Pakistan and CAI logo images courtesy of Central Asia Institute.

70–71
Buy Fresh Buy Local campaign. Designed by Design for Social Impact in collaboration with Food Routes Network.

72–73
Idea Store, Whitechapel images © London Borough of Tower Hamlets.

Chapter 4

78
The Hay Wain (1821) by John Constable image courtesy of The Art Archive / National Gallery London / Eileen Tweedy.

80
Climate Change Poster "They Already Know". The material on page 80 is reproduced with the permission of Oxfam GB, Oxfam House, John Smith Drive, Cowley, Oxford OX4 2JY, UK www.oxfam.org.uk. Oxfam GB does not necessarily endorse any text or activities that accompany the materials.

84–85
United Nations Human Development Index map of the world courtesy of www.undp.org.

86–87
Changing Habbits designed and developed by Professor Rob Holdway and Professor David Walker of Giraffe Innovation.

88–89
BioRegional's 'One Planet Living' flower and One Planet logotype courtesy of BioRegional Development Group.

90–91
'I'm NOT a plastic bag' and 'I am a plastic bag and I'm 100% recyclable' © We Are What We Do.

99
Forum for the Future logotype courtesy of Forum for the Future.

Chapter 5

105
Remarkable Recycled Pencil © Remarkable Ltd. All rights reserved (2010).

109
LCA tool screen capture © 2008-2010 Sustainable Minds, LLC. All rights reserved.

110
Climatex images © Gessner AG.

111
Embody Chair image © 2010 Herman Miller, Inc.

113
InterFLOR images © InterfaceFLOR Europe Ltd.

114
Plan A images © 2010 Marks and Spencer plc.

117
'From sustainability in design to design in sustainability' adapted from 'Ecological Habits of Mind'. Courtesy of Emma Dewberry and Kate Fletcher.

Chapter 6

120
DIY Kyoto's Wattson energy meter © DIY Kyoto.

123
Vélib' cycle hire scheme © Alexey U. Courtesy of www.shutterstock.com.

126–127
Beddington Zero Energy Development images © BioRegional.

128–129
The Powerful Green Map of NYC provided by Green Map System.

132–133
Earth Market research stall photos by Anna Meroni and Mauro Zambetta.

135
Freiburg, self-styled 'green' city courtesy of Crazy D.

136–137
Brixton Pound © 2009, Transition Town Brixton (design by Rob Adderley).

140
DaSH project courtesy of Design Council (UK).

Chapter 7

150
Out of Poverty images courtesy of IDE www.paulpolak.com.

152–153
Mother Earth images courtesy of Hannah Padgett.

154
LifeStraw – Design for the other 90% © Vestergaard Frandsen SA.

156–157
Motivation photograph © David Constantine, Motivation.

158–159
IDEO's Human-Centered Design Toolkit © Courtesy of IDEO.

160–161
Architecture for Humanity UK: The Crisis Christmas project courtesy of Architecture for Humanity UK, London Chapter.

162
The Rest Saving the West © Carolina Vallejo, Design for the First World.

164
Wood carvers in Mandalay and Thai pots images courtesy of John Ballyn.

All reasonable attempts have been made to trace, clear and credit the copyright holders of the images reproduced in this book. However, if any credits have been inadvertently omitted, the publisher will endeavour to incorporate amendments in future editions.

Thanks

Dedications

Anne: I want to dedicate this book to my husband Colin Webb and my mum and dad Bernie and Maureen Chick.

Paul: I want to dedicate this book to my dad, Roy. He would've been proud.

Thanks

Georgia and Caroline at AVA Publishing for their endless patience and support throughout this project. Kathryn Best for proposing us to AVA as the authors for their first book on the subject of design for sustainability. To the 2008/09, 2009/10 and 2010/11 students of the MA Design for Development course at Kingston University who have generously given of their opinions and knowledge in the development of the book's content.

All these people have helped us to develop the ideas presented in this book, through collaboration or conversation.

Jason Allcorn
Mark Ballance
Tracy Bhamra
Charlotte Coetzee
Alastair Fuad-Luke
Michael Herrmann
Rosie Hornbuckle
Chris Horrocks
Sarah Johnson
Andrew Kennedy
Hannah Padgett
Miles Park
Mike Press
Lauren Tan
Stuart Walker

Publisher's note

The subject of ethics is not new, yet its consideration within the applied visual arts is perhaps not as prevalent as it might be. Our aim here is to help a new generation of students, educators and practitioners find a methodology for structuring their thoughts and reflections in this vital area.

AVA Publishing hopes that these **Working with ethics** pages provide a platform for consideration and a flexible method for incorporating ethical concerns in the work of educators, students and professionals. Our approach consists of four parts:

The **introduction** is intended to be an accessible snapshot of the ethical landscape, both in terms of historical development and current dominant themes.

A selection of **further reading** for you to consider areas of particular interest in more detail.

The **framework** positions ethical consideration into four areas and poses questions about the practical implications that might occur. Marking your response to each of these questions on the scale shown will allow your reactions to be further explored by comparison.

The **case study** sets out a real project and then poses some ethical questions for further consideration. This is a focus point for a debate rather than a critical analysis so there are no predetermined right or wrong answers.

Required Reading Range
Working with ethics

Lynne Elvins and
Naomi Goulder

Introduction

Ethics is a complex subject that interlaces the idea of responsibilities to society with a wide range of considerations relevant to the character and happiness of the individual. It concerns virtues of compassion, loyalty and strength, but also of confidence, imagination, humour and optimism. As introduced in ancient Greek philosophy, the fundamental ethical question is: *what should I do?* How we might pursue a 'good' life not only raises moral concerns about the effects of our actions on others, but also personal concerns about our own integrity.

In modern times the most important and controversial questions in ethics have been the moral ones. With growing populations and improvements in mobility and communications, it is not surprising that considerations about how to structure our lives together on the planet should come to the forefront. For visual artists and communicators, it should be no surprise that these considerations will enter into the creative process.

Some ethical considerations are already enshrined in government laws and regulations or in professional codes of conduct. For example, plagiarism and breaches of confidentiality can be punishable offences. Legislation in various nations makes it unlawful to exclude people with disabilities from accessing information or spaces. The trade of ivory as a material has been banned in many countries. In these cases, a clear line has been drawn under what is unacceptable.

But most ethical matters remain open to debate, among experts and lay-people alike, and in the end we have to make our own choices on the basis of our own guiding principles or values. Is it more ethical to work for a charity than for a commercial company? Is it unethical to create something that others find ugly or offensive?

Specific questions such as these may lead to other questions that are more abstract. For example, is it only effects on humans (and what they care about) that are important, or might effects on the natural world require attention too?

Is promoting ethical consequences justified even when it requires ethical sacrifices along the way? Must there be a single unifying theory of ethics (such as the Utilitarian thesis that the right course of action is always the one that leads to the greatest happiness of the greatest number), or might there always be many different ethical values that pull a person in various directions?

As we enter into ethical debate and engage with these dilemmas on a personal and professional level, we may change our views or change our view of others. The real test though is whether, as we reflect on these matters, we change the way we act as well as the way we think. Socrates, the 'father' of philosophy, proposed that people will naturally do 'good' if they know what is right. But this point might only lead us to yet another question: *how do we know what is right?*

Further reading

AIGA
Design Business and Ethics
2007, AIGA

Eaton, Marcia Muelder
Aesthetics and the Good Life
1989, Associated University Press

Ellison, David
Ethics and Aesthetics in European Modernist Literature: From the Sublime to the Uncanny
2001, Cambridge University Press

Fenner, David E W (Ed)
Ethics and the Arts: An Anthology
1995, Garland Reference Library of Social Science

Gini, Al and Marcoux, Alexei M *Case Studies in Business Ethics*
2005, Prentice Hall

McDonough, William and Braungart, Michael
Cradle to Cradle: Remaking the Way We Make Things
2002, North Point Press

Papanek, Victor
Design for the Real World: Making to Measure
1972, Thames & Hudson

United Nations Global Compact
The Ten Principles
www.unglobalcompact.org/aboutthegc/thetenprinciples/index.html